10 MINUTE GUIDE TO Lotus Approach®

Robert Mullen

alpha books

A Division of Macmillan Computer Publishing
201 West 103rd Street, Indianapolis, Indiana 46290 USA

©1994 by Alpha Books

All rights reserved. No part of this book shall be reproduced, stored in a retrieval system, or transmitted by any means, electronic, mechanical, photocopying, recording, or otherwise, without written permission from the publisher. No patent liability is assumed with respect to the use of the information contained herein. Although every precaution has been taken in the preparation of this book, the publisher and author assume no responsibility for errors or omissions. Neither is any liability assumed for damages resulting from the use of the information contained herein. For information, address Alpha Books, 201 W. 103rd Street, Indianapolis, IN 46290.

International Standard Book Number: 1-56761-407-8
Library of Congress Catalog Card Number: 93-73710

96   95   94   8   7   6   5   4   3   2   1

Interpretation of the printing code: the rightmost number of the first series of numbers is the year of the book's printing; the rightmost number of the second series of numbers is the number of the book's printing. For example, a printing code of 94-1 shows that the first printing of the book occurred in 1994.

Screen reproductions in this book were created by means of the program Collage Plus from Inner Media, Inc., Hollis, NH.

Printed in the United States of America

Publisher: Marie Butler-Knight
Managing Editor: Elizabeth Keaffaber
Product Development Manager: Faithe Wempen
Acquisitions Manager: Barry Pruett
Production Editor: Phil Kitchel
Copy Editor: Audra Gable
Book Designer: Barbara Webster
Cover Design: Sandra Stevenson
Indexer: Bront Davis
Production: Gary Adair, Dan Caparo, Brad Chinn, Kim Cofer, Lisa Daugherty, Jennifer Eberhardt, Mark Enochs, Beth Rago, Bobbi Satterfield, Kris Simmons, Carol Stamile, Robert Wolf

Special thanks to C. Herbert Feltner for ensuring the technical accuracy of this book.

Contents

Introduction, vi

1 How Approach Works, 1
Some Basic Terms, 1
Approach Databases and Forms, 2
Approach's Presentation Power, 3

2 Starting and Exiting Lotus Approach, 7
Starting Lotus Approach, 7
What You'll See, 8
Quitting Lotus Approach, 9

3 Navigating the Approach Screen, 11
Basic Approach Screen Elements, 11
View Tabs, 14

4 Using SmartIcons, 16
What Are SmartIcons?, 16

5 Getting Help, 23
Help Is Available!, 23
Context-Sensitive Help, 23
Bubble Help, 24
The Help Menu, 25

6 Approach Views, 30
Approach's Many Views, 30
What About Modes?, 36

7 Creating and Saving a Database, 37
Creating a Database, 37
Getting Information About a Saved File, 42

8 Opening Existing Files, 44
Opening an Approach File, 44

9 Importing and Exporting Information, 52
Why Import and Export?, 52
Importing Data, 52
Exporting Information, 55
Exporting for Your Word Processor, 57

10 Adding Records to a Database, 59

11 Finding, Editing, and Deleting Records, 62
Finding Records, 62
Changing Records, 67
Deleting Records, 67

12 Sorting Your Records, 69
Approach's Powerful Sorting Capabilities, 69
Sorting in Form View, 71
Sorting in Worksheet View, 71
Custom Sorting, 72

13 Creating Reports and Worksheets, 74
Creating a Report, 74
Creating Additional Worksheets, 77

14 Mailing Labels and Form Letters, 79
Making Mailing Labels, 79
Creating a Form Letter, 82
Using a Form Letter, 85

15 Creating a Chart, 88
Creating a Chart, 88

16 Creating a Form, 91
Creating a Form, 92

17 Working with Design Mode, 96
Entering Design Mode, 96
Selecting an Object, 98
Moving an Object, 99
Resizing an Object, 100
Editing Text, 101

18 Adding Graphics to a View, 103
Drawing Your Own Graphic Objects, 103
Importing Graphics from Other Programs, 106
Deleting Graphics, 108
Placing OLE Graphics in a View, 108
Creating Stacked Graphics, 111

Contents v

19 Making Your Forms Easier to Use, 113
Changing the Tab Order of the Fields, 113
Using an InfoBox to Format Fields, 115
Creating Radio Buttons, 116
Aligning Fields on a Form, 117

20 Printing Your Data, 120
Previewing before Printing, 120
Printing a View, 121
Changing the Print Setup, 123

21 Working with Numbers, 126
Summarizing, 126
Using Calculated Fields, 128

22 Validating Data Input, 133
Minimizing Data Entry Errors with Validated Fields, 133
Types of Validation, 134
Setting Up Field Validation, 135

23 Joining Files, 137
Different Types of Database Programs, 137
Joining Approach Files, 137
Joining Records with Repeating Panels, 140

24 Running Macros to Save Time, 143
Creating New Macros, 143
Using Existing Macros, 146
Editing a Macro, 146

A SmartIcons, 149

B Windows Primer, 155
Starting Microsoft Windows, 155
Using a Mouse, 156
Starting a Program, 158
Using Menus, 158
Navigating Dialog Boxes, 159
Switching Between Windows, 161
Controlling a Window, 161

Introduction

I'm a list maker. I always have been. Until recently, I even made lists to keep track of other lists! I had lists of people, dates, events, places, account information, phone numbers—and of lists I should be making. I stacked them all up on either side of my computer, rummaging through them when I needed some info.

Long ago, I also got into the habit of relying on a hard copy record-keeping system that had no real room for expansion (like when I ran out of lines on the page where info about the Joneses was kept). If I had too many Joneses, I had to add another blank page for the letter "J." What a nightmare!

And then I found Lotus Approach.

What Is Lotus Approach?

Lotus Approach is a forms-based database management system (DBMS). What you see on your screen is what you see on paper—including data entry forms. Forms make the job of information management simple because the data entry screens that you use look just like the paper form.

> **Database Management System (DBMS)** A program that allows you to collect, organize, and review large amounts of well-ordered information.
>
> *Plain English*

Many of the most popular database programs in past years have been rather unfriendly to use, relying on cryptic prompts and commands. Lotus Approach is a new breed of database program. It's a very graphical program based on

Microsoft Windows, and it relies on simple menus and buttons instead of typed commands. You don't have to learn a programming language or know what's inside your computer's box. You simply select from menus (lists) of available options and commands.

Another big difference between Lotus Approach and the more traditional DBMS products is what you are able to do with the data you enter. In text-based database programs, your data appeared in a long list. To create an effective display of your data, you had to export it to a graphics presentation program. This lack of presentation power made most traditional DBMS products a pain to get onto paper in a meaningful fashion, since the user had to be good at using yet another software product that was designed to present database information in printed or viewable form.

Lotus Approach enables you to work with your information as though it were a more traditional "table" of data; but the real power of Approach lies in its presentation ability. You can actually access, add to, delete, and change information while viewing it in the final, printed format, such as a report on your company's letterhead.

What Will This Book Teach Me?

This book teaches you only what you *need* to know in order to quickly become productive with Lotus Approach. You can learn how to:

- Create your own databases.
- Sort information in your preferred order.
- Find stored information fast!
- Create customized, printed reports.
- Import and export other database and spreadsheet information.
- Create charts and graphs.

With Approach, you can combine information from different sources, such as your favorite spreadsheet or the database on the network. You can export Approach's information in popular file formats like dBASE, FoxPro, and Paradox. And you can link data from other applications while they're running to keep the information in your Approach database files current.

How to Use the 10 Minute Guide

Each of the short lessons in the *10 Minute Guide to Lotus Approach* include step-by-step instructions for performing some specific task. The following special icons are included as a way to help you quickly identify particular types of information:

Plain English This icon appears wherever a new term is defined. Watch for this symbol to help you learn the terms you need in order to understand Lotus Approach and learn more about how it works.

Panic Button This icon appears next to areas where new users might run into trouble. Watch for this symbol to help you avoid making mistakes.

Timesaver Tip This icon offers shortcuts and hints on how to most effectively use the ideas presented. Watch for this symbol to identify ways to save time when using Lotus Approach.

In addition, you'll see the following conventions used to organize the book's material.

1.	Numbered steps provide exact instructions for frequently needed procedures.
Acme Corporation	Information you must type appears in bold, colored type.
Things you select	Menu names, commands, or options you must select appear in colored type.
On-screen text	Messages that are displayed on-screen appear in bold.
Key combinations	In many cases, you must press a two-key combination in order to enter a command. For example, "Press Alt+X" means to hold down the first key and press the second key.

Acknowledgments

Many individuals contributed their knowledge and experience to this book. I would like to thank Matt Wagner at Waterside. At Alpha Books, I would like to thank Faithe Wempen, Phil Kitchel, Audra Gable, and Herb Feltner.

Trademarks

All terms mentioned in this book that are known to be trademarks or service marks are listed below. In addition, terms suspected of being trademarks or service marks have been appropriately capitalized. Alpha Books cannot attest to the accuracy of this information. Use of a term in this book should not be regarded as affecting the validity of any trademark or service mark.

MS-DOS and Windows are trademarks of Microsoft Corporation.

FoxPro is a registered trademark of Microsoft Corporation.

Lotus Approach is a registered trademark of Lotus Development Corporation.

Lotus SmartSuite is a registered trademark of Lotus Development Corporation.

Lotus 1-2-3 is a registered trademark of Lotus Development Corporation.

dBASE is a registered trademark of Borland International Incorporated.

Oracle is a registered trademark of Oracle Corporation.

Paradox is a registered trademark of Borland International Incorporated.

Lesson 1

How Approach Works

In this lesson, you'll learn the basics about using Lotus Approach.

Lotus Approach is one of a new breed of database management systems. Unlike many database programs that force you to work mainly with long lists, Approach is designed to present information as you actually use it: in forms that resemble printed documents, charts, worksheets, and so on.

> **Forms Management** Presenting information as it will eventually appear on paper is called *forms management*.
>
> *Plain English*

Approach allows you to work with your data as if you were working on the same printed documents you might use or distribute to others. You are insulated from the actual databases you create and use, and you don't have to have any programming knowledge. Approach gives you the means to view and work with your information in virtually every popular format. You can view your information as though it were a spreadsheet, lists of records, paper-based forms, conventional and customized reports, and even form letters.

Some Basic Terms

A *database* is a collection of facts and figures. The data is organized in rows and columns, forming a table. A *field* is a category of information that you have for each person or item represented, such as an Address, Title, or ID Number.

Fields normally form the column headings in the data table. A *record* is a collection of all the facts and figures relating to a single person or item. For instance, the Name, Title, Address, and ID Number of a single employee might form a single record (or row) in a personnel database.

A *form* is a mask that's placed over the database to shield you from dealing directly with long, unappealing lists. The form displays a single record at a time on the screen, with the fields arranged in some logical fashion that makes it easy to use the data. You can move from one record to the next using the keyboard or mouse, as you'll learn in Lesson 6.

Approach Databases and Forms

In many popular database management programs, everything is stored in a single file—your data, your forms, your formatting information, and so on. This makes it difficult to share your data with others who use different programs, since the file is in a proprietary format.

In Approach, forms are stored separately from the databases they pertain to. Form files end in an .APR extension. Database files can be maintained in any of several popular formats, including dBASE III+ or IV, Paradox 3.5 and 4.0, and FoxPro 2.1. This ensures that you can easily share your data with people who use other database programs, if necessary.

A single database can employ many different forms. Each form provides a different *view* (a different way of seeing your information). When you create a new database, you have the option of assigning a ready-made form to it, complete with predefined fields, or of creating your own form. You'll learn to create a new database in Lesson 6.

How Approach Works

Auto-Attach When you open an existing database, you automatically open the associated forms with it—you don't have to worry about opening the forms separately each time. You'll learn more about opening existing database files in Lesson 7.

Approach's Presentation Power

Forms provide an easy way to enter and edit data, but at times you may want to do more than just look at your data on-screen. Approach gives you the power to see your information in any of several formats, including charts, worksheets, mailing labels, form letters, and reports.

Charts

A *chart* (also called a *graph*) is a graphical display of information. Lotus Approach helps you create charts in 2-D and 3-D and in full color.

Want to Print in Color? Of course, you need a color printer in order to print charts in color!

Approach can help you create several types of charts, including bar, line, area, and pie. For each of these basic types of charts, you can choose from several variations on the basic chart. Figure 1.1 shows you how you might use a pie chart to show how several components add up to an overall total.

Approach provides you with a Chart Assistant to help you create charts easily and quickly. Chart Assistant steps you through the process of creating your charts, helping you make choices at every point along the way.

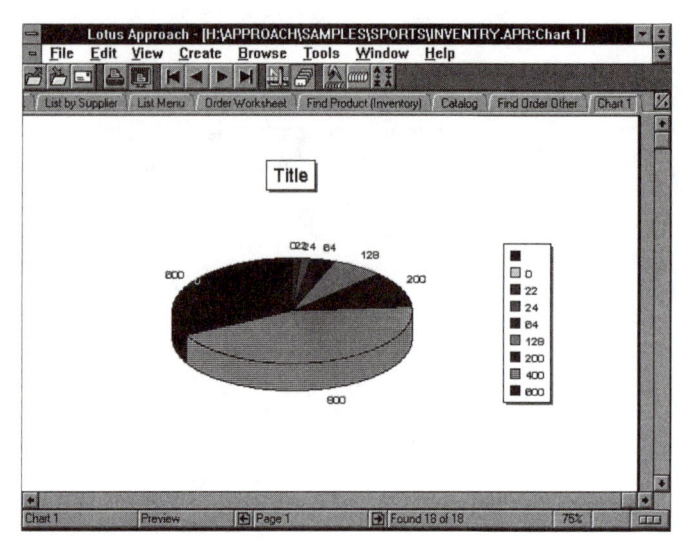

Figure 1.1 A simple 3-D pie chart.

Worksheets

A *worksheet* is a collection of information that's visually organized into columns and rows. Rows run from left to right across your screen. Columns stretch from top to bottom. Each column represents a field in the database, and each row represents a record.

Mailing Labels

A *mailing label* contains information from your database that is used to mail packages or letters. Typically, names, addresses, city, state, and ZIP code information comprise the printed text of a mailing label.

   Approach creates mailing labels for you. Either you can use the default Mailing Label style or you can create a custom mailing label. If you decide to create a custom mailing label, Approach provides you with a Mailing Label Assistant to step you through the process. Mailing Label Assistant offers three

How Approach Works

Lotus Approach table

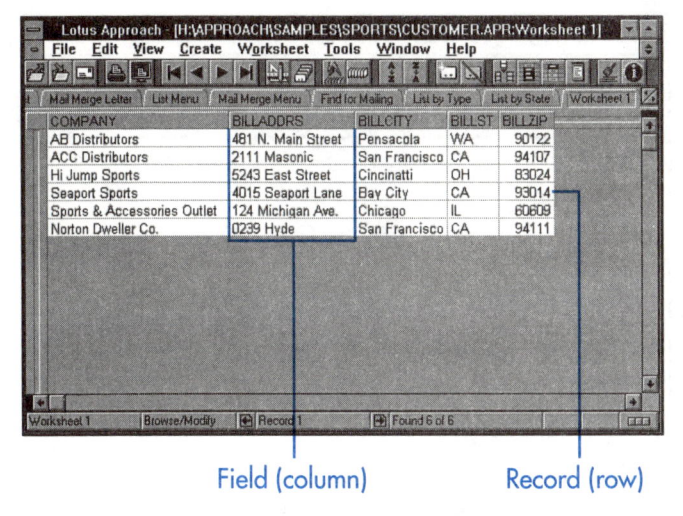

Field (column)   Record (row)

Figure 1.2 An example of a small worksheet.

basic mailing label layouts. You can select one of these layouts, or you can create a unique layout that suits your particular needs.

Form Letters

A *form letter* combines information from your database with text that you type onto a standard letter, and you use one when you need to send the same message to multiple recipients. If you have mailing address information stored in a database, Approach can help you create a form letter for each person represented in that database.

Reports

When you need to present lots of information on the fewest pages, you will probably want to use a report to do so. A *report* displays multiple records on a single page. You can sort information alphabetically or numerically by any field. You can total columns of figures, and even total subtotals from other pages of the same report. Figure 1.3 shows you a basic report, detailing a retailer's inventory status.

Lesson 1

```
Lotus Approach - [H:\APPROACH\SAMPLES\SPORTS\INVENTRY.APR:Current Inventory]
 File  Edit  View  Create  Browse  Tools  Window  Help

 Our Current Inventory Status
    ITEMNO   RECEIVE   SOLD     INVNO   DATE
    JSP040              0                12/2/91
    DC088                        102    1/11/93
    JSP040             200       102
    RC022                        102    1/11/92
    JSP040             400       103
    ASW92                        101    1/13/93
    JSP040             128       101
    DC088     100                       1/14/94
    DC088              22        101
    DC088              24        106
    DC088     0
    JSP040    40                        12/6/91
    DC088              400       102
    RC022              600       102
    ASW92              64        101
    JF82169   0        0                12/7/92
    DC088                        102
    Wednesday, May 04, 1994
```

Figure 1.3 A simple report.

You can place a *header* at the top of each printed page of your report, or you can place a *footer* at the bottom of each page. Headers and footers can include such information as your company's name, today's date, or the page number. Figure 1.3 shows a worksheet with the current date as the footer. You can select just what you want to see at the top and bottom of each page of your report.

In this lesson, you learned the ways you can use Lotus Approach to work with information. In the next lesson, you'll learn how to start and exit Lotus Approach.

Lesson 2

Starting and Exiting Lotus Approach

In this lesson, you'll learn how to start and leave Lotus Approach.

Starting Lotus Approach

Before you start Approach, you must have installed it, and Windows must be running. (For instructions on installing the program, see the inside front cover of this book.) If you are new to the Windows environment, you'll want to read the appendix "Microsoft Windows Primer" at the back of this book before proceeding.

If you haven't yet started Windows, you'll need to do so by typing **WIN** at the DOS prompt. After a few seconds, the Program Manager window appears on-screen. Here's how you start Lotus Approach from Program Manager:

1. Open the Window menu and select Approach 3.0 for Windows. Figure 2.1 shows you the Approach 3.0 for Windows group window.

2. Double-click on the Approach 3.0 icon.

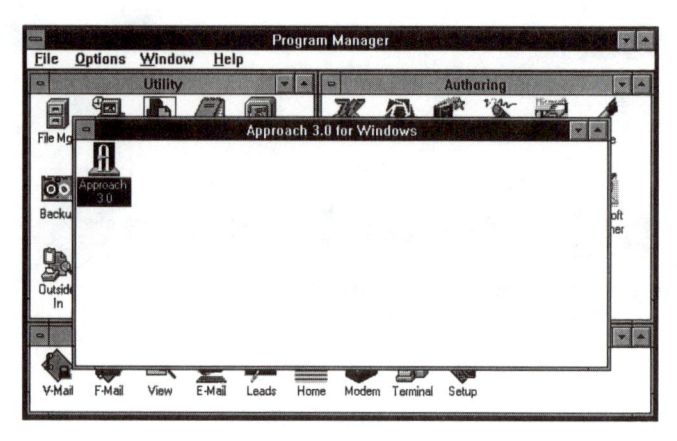

Figure 2.1 The Approach 3.0 for Windows group window.

What You'll See

When you start Approach, you'll see a banner screen that tells you about the user to whom your copy of Approach is registered. You are then presented with a dialog box that offers to help you get started. Figure 2.2 shows you the Welcome to Lotus Approach dialog box.

In the Welcome dialog box, you have the options of opening an existing Approach file (Approach files end with a file name extension of .APR) or creating a new Approach file (either blank or based on an existing template). For now, click on **Cancel**, because we're not ready to do any of these things yet.

> **Avoiding the Welcome** You can click on the Don't show this screen again check box if you want to disable the Welcome to Lotus Approach dialog box. If you do so, the next time you start Approach, a plain screen will appear (see the background of Figure 2.3) instead of the dialog box.

Starting and Exiting Lotus Approach

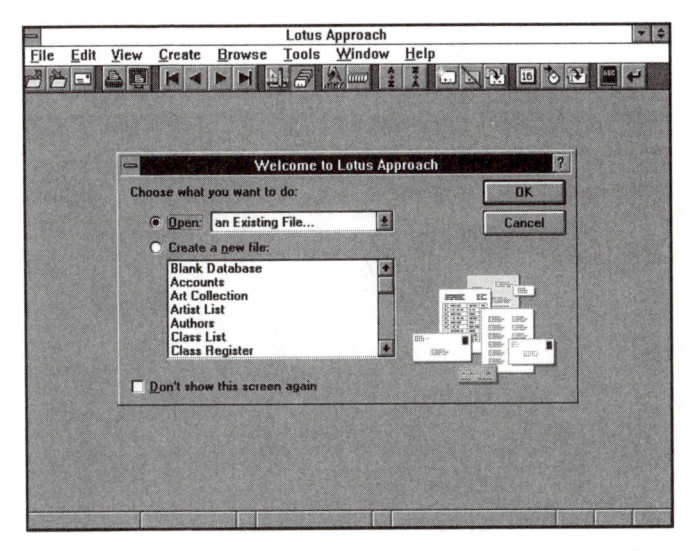

Figure 2.2 The Welcome to Lotus Approach dialog box.

Quitting Lotus Approach

There may be times when you want to quit using Approach, but you know that you will be coming back to it later. If so, you should exit from Approach. You can do so using either of these methods:

- Double-click on Approach's Control-menu box

  or

- Open the File menu and select Exit. (If you don't know how to open and use menus, see the Microsoft Windows Primer at the back of this book.)

Figure 2.3 shows both methods of exiting Approach.

Lesson 2

Double-click the
Control-menu box.

```
Quit Approach and prompt to save all unsaved files
File  Edit  View  Create  Browse  Tools  Window  Help
  New...
  Open...            Ctrl+O
  Close
  Save Approach File  Ctrl+S
  Save As...
  Delete File...
  Import Data...
  Export Data...
  Approach File Info...
  Send Mail...
  Preview            Ctrl+Shift+B
  Print...           Ctrl+P
  Print Setup...
  Exit
  1 ORDERS.APR
  2 INVENTRY.APR
```

Or, open the   ...and select the Exit
File menu...   command.

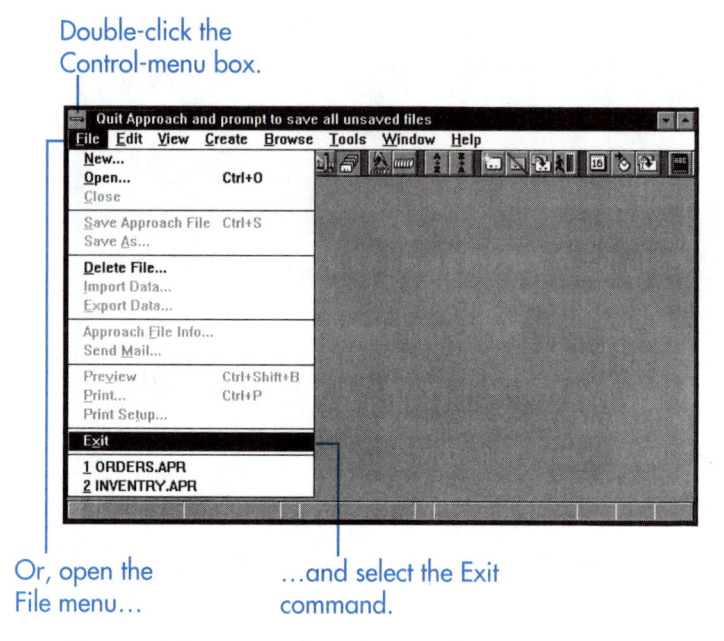

Figure 2.3 Exiting from Approach.

If any files are open and have not yet been saved, Lotus Approach will prompt you to save them. That's why it's important to leave the application in one of the three ways just listed: Approach has the chance to save any new or changed information. Never just turn off the computer!

In this lesson, you learned how to start and exit Approach. In the next lesson, you'll learn about the screens you'll see as you work with your database files.

Lesson 3

Navigating the Approach Screen

In this lesson, you'll learn about the parts of the Approach screen and how to use them to control your databases.

> **It's a Lot Like Windows** Approach's application window is made up of all of the usual Windows screen objects, such as the Control-menu box, title bar, minimize and maximize buttons, window border, and Approach's main menu. Turn to the appendix, "Microsoft Windows Primer" to learn more about Windows.

Basic Approach Screen Elements

Some elements appear in every Approach window, whether a database is open or not (for example, the menu bar, SmartIcons, and the status bar). Let's look at these basic parts first, since you'll be working with them all the time.

Figure 3.1 shows the Approach screen with no Approach file open. Of course, you can't do any work without opening a file or creating a new one, but for now let's just look at the basic screen elements.

Lesson 3

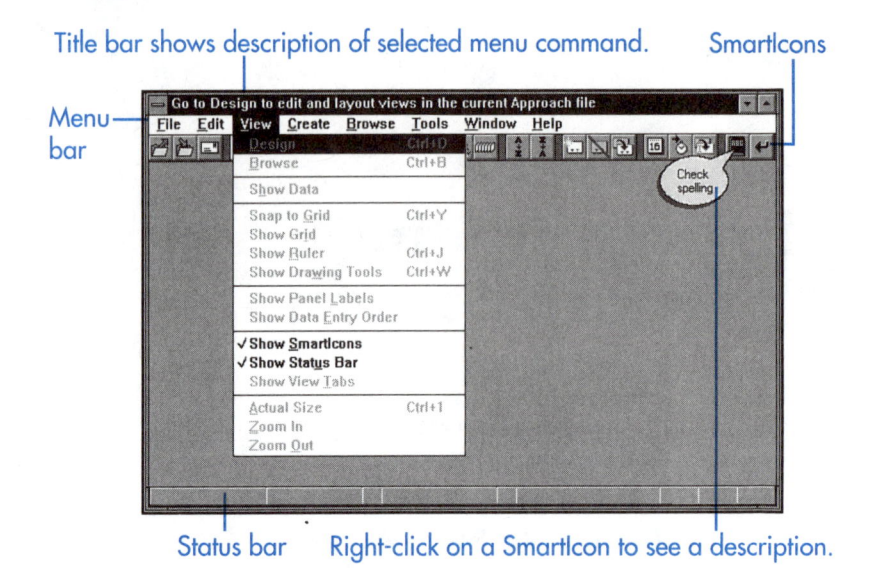

Figure 3.1 annotations: Title bar shows description of selected menu command. SmartIcons. Menu bar. Status bar. Right-click on a SmartIcon to see a description.

Figure 3.1 The basic screen elements of Lotus Approach.

Title Bar

The *title bar* runs across the top of the window. When nothing is going on, the title bar displays the title of the program: Lotus Approach. When a file is open, its name appears there too. When a menu is open and a command is selected, the title bar gives a description of the command.

Menu Bar

Immediately below the title bar is Approach's *menu bar*. Approach's menus are organized much as they are in any other Windows application. Menu names appear in a horizontal bar across the width of Approach's screen. Click on any of these menu names to open the menu, and then select any item on that menu by clicking on it.

Navigating the Approach Screen

To open a menu using the keyboard, hold down the **Alt** key and press the underlined letter in the menu's name. Once the menu is open, you can press the underlined letter in a command's name to select it, or use the up and down arrow keys to highlight the command and press **Enter**.

SmartIcons

Just below the menu bar, *SmartIcons* are arranged in a horizontal bar. SmartIcons look like buttons with pictures on them. They provide shortcuts to performing common tasks, such as saving, printing, and sorting. You'll learn more about SmartIcons in Lesson 4.

> **SmartIcons** SmartIcons are buttons that represent common commands you can execute. To use a SmartIcon, click on it.

To find out what a SmartIcon does, right-click on the SmartIcon you're interested in. A bubble appears next to the SmartIcon, explaining its function (as shown in Figure 3.1). Figure 3.2 shows the default SmartIcon set—the ones that appear when you first install Approach.

Figure 3.2 Approach's SmartIcons.

Status Bar

The *status bar* runs along the bottom of Approach's window. It displays such information as the current record number and the view that is in use. (In Figure 3.1 there is no information in the status bar because there is no file open.)

View Tabs

In Lesson 1, you learned that you can create different views for your data. (You'll learn more about the various views in later lessons.) When you create a view for any Approach file, a "folder" style tab appears just below the SmartIcon bar to represent that view. Figure 3.3 shows an example database that contains several *view tabs*. Click on any view tab to activate that view.

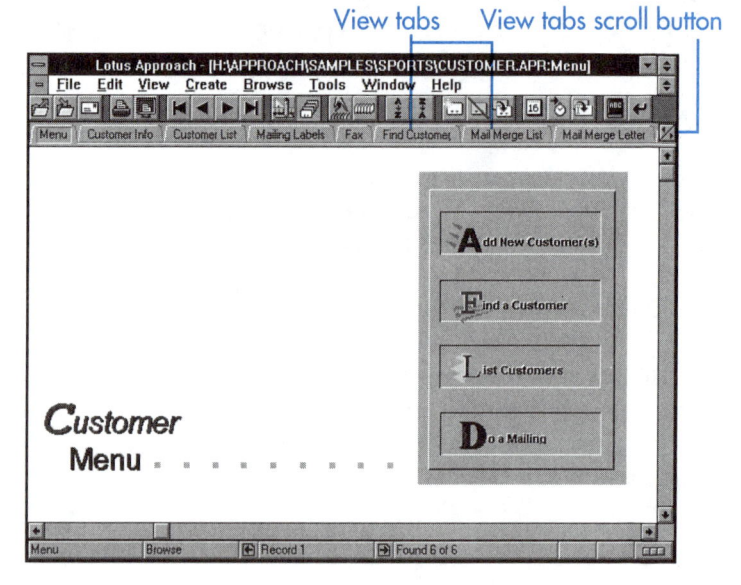

Figure 3.3 An Approach file with many view tabs.

Want to See It Now? You'll learn to create and open databases in Lessons 6 and 7. If you want to see the database shown in Figure 3.3 on your screen now, open the File menu and select Open. Change to the \APPROACH\SAMPLES\SPORTS directory and open the file CUSTOMER.APR. (Skip ahead to Lesson 7 for instructions on opening a file, if necessary.)

If you've created several views for an Approach file, you may have more view tabs than can be displayed at one time. When you have more view tabs that can be displayed at once, a button appears at the far right side of the view tabs (see Figure 3.3). The button has two arrows on it. Click on either arrow to scroll the view tabs to the right and left so you can see them all when you need to.

In this lesson, you learned about Approach's screen elements. In the next lesson, you'll learn more about SmartIcons.

Lesson 4

Using SmartIcons

In this lesson, you'll learn to use Approach's SmartIcons and organize them to fit the way you work.

What Are SmartIcons?

You were introduced briefly to SmartIcons in the previous lesson. SmartIcons look like standard three-dimensional buttons with small pictures on them. Each one represents a common task you can perform, such as opening a file or sorting a list from A to Z.

When you first install Approach, a default set of SmartIcons appears on the SmartIcon bar directly below the menu bar. Table 4.1 shows the default SmartIcons (the Default Browse set is the official name of the set) and tells what they do.

Table 4.1 The Default SmartIcons.

SmartIcon	Function
	Opens a file.
	Saves an Approach file.
	Sends mail.
	Prints current view.
	Prints preview.
	Goes to first record.

Using SmartIcons

SmartIcon	Function
◀	Goes to previous record.
▶	Goes to next record.
▶│	Goes to last record.
	Changes to Design view.
	Changes to Browse view.
	Finds a set of records.
	Finds all records in the database.
A↕Z	Sorts field in ascending order.
Z↕A	Sorts field in descending order.
	Creates a new record.
	Deletes the current record.
	Duplicates the current record.
16	Inserts the current date.
	Inserts the current time.
	Duplicates data from previous record.
ABC	Checks spelling.
↵	Enters the record or performs the find operation.

To select a SmartIcon, simply click on it. Most SmartIcons are used in place of a menu command. For example, you use the Open SmartIcon instead of selecting the Open command from the File menu.

Lesson 4

> **No Keyboard Steps?** There is no procedure for selecting SmartIcons with the keyboard; you must use the mouse.

Customizing the SmartIcon Bar

You can add and remove SmartIcons from the SmartIcon bar so that it reflects the tasks you perform most frequently. You can also create your own customized SmartIcons sets, so you can use different SmartIcon bars for different purposes or with different Approach files.

Changing the Contents of a SmartIcon Set

Approach comes with only one SmartIcon set—Default Browse. You can make changes to this set, so that your custom setup becomes the default, or you can leave Default Browse the way it is and create your own SmartIcon set with a different name. Either way, you start by opening the SmartIcons dialog box. Follow these steps:

1. Select SmartIcons from the Tools menu. The SmartIcons dialog box appears (see Figure 4.1).

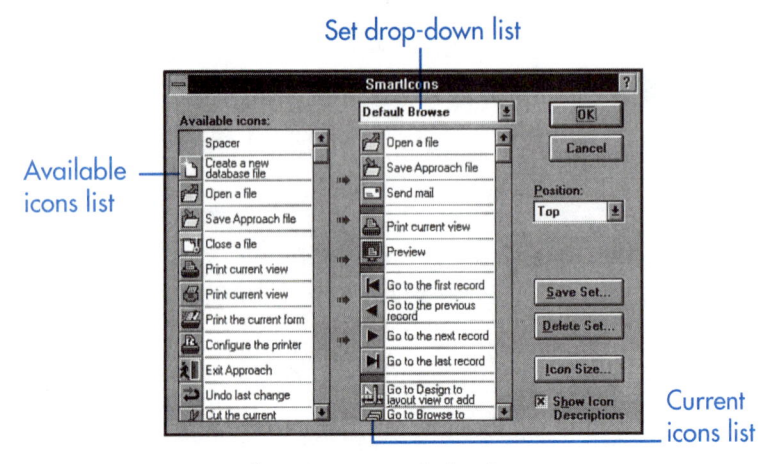

Figure 4.1 The SmartIcons dialog box.

Using SmartIcons

2. Select the SmartIcon set you want to change from the Set drop-down list at the top of the dialog box. If you have not yet created any new sets, there is only one choice: Default Browse.

I Don't Want To Change the Default Set! Don't worry—even though you are about to make changes to a perfectly good SmartIcon set, you'll have the opportunity in step 6 to save the changes under a different name, leaving the original icon set intact.

3. To add an icon to the current SmartIcon set, drag any icon from the Available icons list to the point where you want the icon to appear on the Current icons list.

4. To delete an icon from the current SmartIcon set, drag the icon from the Current icons list to any point on the Available icons list.

5. If you want to overwrite the old SmartIcon set with the changes you've made, click OK, and you're done. If you want to save the set under a different name, go on to step 6.

6. Click the Save Set button. The Save Set of SmartIcons dialog box appears (Figure 4.2).

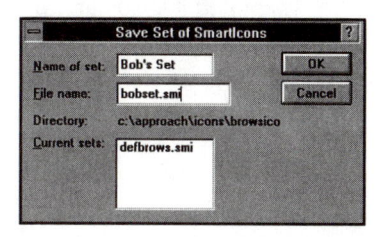

Figure 4.2 The Save Set of SmartIcons dialog box.

7. Type a description of the new set in the Name of set text box, and type a file name for it in the File name text box.

8. Click OK to save the SmartIcon set.

9. Click OK to close the SmartIcons dialog box.

Rearranging SmartIcons

You can rearrange SmartIcons if the order in which they currently appear is not convenient for you. To do this, return to the SmartIcons dialog box. Here are the steps:

1. Select SmartIcons from the Tools menu. The SmartIcons dialog box appears (Figure 4.1).

2. To move a SmartIcon to a different place in the current SmartIcon set, drag any icon from its current position on the Current icons list to the desired location.

3. Click OK when you're finished rearranging icons.

> **Make Space!** You can move a space around just like any other SmartIcon! A Spacer icon appears at the top of the Available icons list (see Figure 4.1). Simply drag it to wherever you want a space to appear on the SmartIcon bar. To add more spaces, add the Spacer icon just as you would add any other icon (see "Changing the Contents of a SmartIcon Set" earlier in this lesson).

Deleting Entire Sets of SmartIcons

You can delete an entire SmartIcon set if you want to. You might want to do this, for example, if you created a special SmartIcon set for a specific project, and the project has come to a close.

Here's how you delete an entire SmartIcon set:

1. Select SmartIcons from the Tools menu. The SmartIcons dialog box appears (Figure 4.1).

2. Click the Delete Set button, and the Delete Sets dialog box appears.

3. Click on the name of the SmartIcon set you want to delete, and then click on the OK button to delete the set and close the Delete Sets dialog box. The set is now permanently gone.

4. Click OK to close the SmartIcons dialog box.

> **Oh No!** Approach offers no way to salvage a set you have deleted. It's gone forever. However, if you have DOS 6 or higher or some other utility program, you may be able to use it to get the SmartIcon file back if you act immediately. (See that program's manual for instructions.)

Changing the Position of the SmartIcon Bar

You aren't stuck with displaying the SmartIcon bar along the top of the screen: you can position it along the bottom or either side if you prefer. You can also make the bar a "floating" element that you can drag around on the screen as needed. Here's how:

1. Select SmartIcons from the Tools menu. The SmartIcons dialog box appears.

2. Open the Position drop-down list, and click on any of the position choices.

3. Click OK to close the SmartIcons dialog box. The SmartIcon bar is now displayed in the position you chose. The next time you start Approach, you will

Lesson 4

see that the SmartIcon bar is still in the position in which you placed it. It remains there until you move it again.

Zoom In! You can change the size of the SmartIcons that appear on-screen. Just click on the Icon Size button while the SmartIcons dialog box is open, and select the size you like!

In this lesson, you learned how to customize and reposition Approach's SmartIcon bar. In the next lesson, you'll learn how to get help from Approach.

Lesson 5

Getting Help

In this lesson, you'll learn how to get help when working in Approach.

Help Is Available!

Approach offers a comprehensive Help facility that you can access in a variety of ways.

- For context-sensitive help, press F1 or click the Help SmartIcon.
- For Bubble Help, point and right-click.
- For the Help menu, select Help from the menu bar.

You'll learn more about each of these in the following sections.

Context-Sensitive Help

The easiest way to get help is to press the F1 key, which brings up *context-sensitive help*.

> **Context-Sensitive Help** In context-sensitive help, the information that appears depends on what Approach feature you are using at the time. For example, if you just selected Print from the File menu, and you press F1, information about printing appears.

Some dialog boxes also contain a Help command button. When you select it, you get the same context-sensitive help as if you had pressed F1.

Bubble Help

If you've ever used a Mac, you probably are familiar with "balloon help" (little balloons filled with information that pop up when you need help). Lotus Approach uses a variation of this called *Bubble Help*. Here's how to use it:

1. Point the mouse pointer at the object you're seeking help on.

2. Press and hold the right mouse button while you read the text that appears in the bubble.

Bubble Help is the fastest, simplest way to learn about something you *see* on your screen when using Lotus Approach. Figure 5.1 shows you Bubble Help describing the function of the Help SmartIcon.

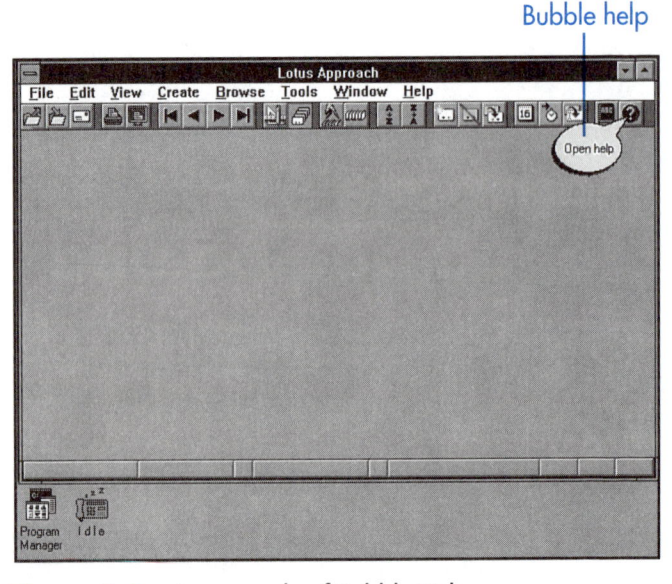

Figure 5.1 An example of Bubble Help.

Bubble Help is available only when your mouse pointer is positioned over a screen element that's part of the Lotus Approach application. If Bubble Help isn't available for an item you need help with, use one of the other methods to access the Help system (press F1, click the Help SmartIcon, or select the Help menu).

The Help Menu

If you have a general question about a topic, or aren't sure how to even begin a task, the Help menu is your best bet. Just click on Help on the menu bar, and a menu of choices drops down.

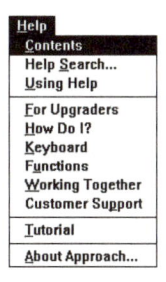

Figure 5.2 Approach's Help menu.

The following sections explain some of the most commonly used options on the Help menu.

Contents

Contents is your main entrance to the Help facility. When you select Contents from the Help menu, the Contents screen appears, as shown in Figure 5.3.

Lesson 5

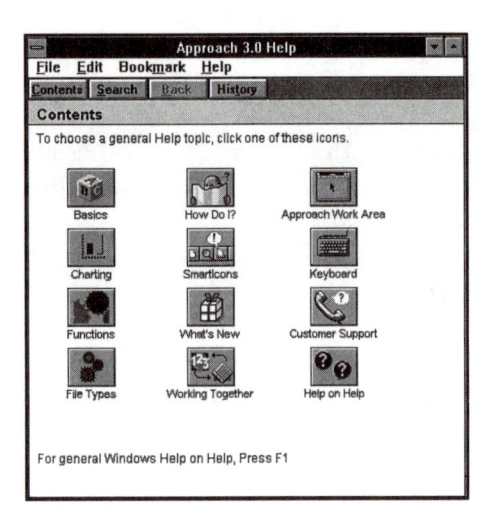

Figure 5.3 The Approach 3.0 Help window.

The Approach 3.0 Help window displays twelve icons that represent more specific topics of interest. Click on any of these twelve icons to get help on Approach Basics, Charting, Functions, and so on.

> **SmartIcon Shortcut** You can also click on the Help SmartIcon to see the Help Contents window. The Help SmartIcon is not displayed by default; you must modify your SmartIcon bar to include it if you want to use it. Refer to Lesson 4 for details on customizing the SmartIcon bar.

After you've clicked on an icon, a list of green underlined topics appears. These are jump words. Clicking on a jump word "jumps" you to information about that topic.

> **Jump Words** Words that jump to more specific information when clicked. Jump words are usually denoted by the use of green text.

Getting Help 27

Help Search

Instead of wading through layers of lists of topics (as you do using the Help Contents command), you can jump directly to the topic that interests you with the Help Search command. Follow these steps:

1. Select Help Search from the Help menu. The Search dialog box appears (Figure 5.4).

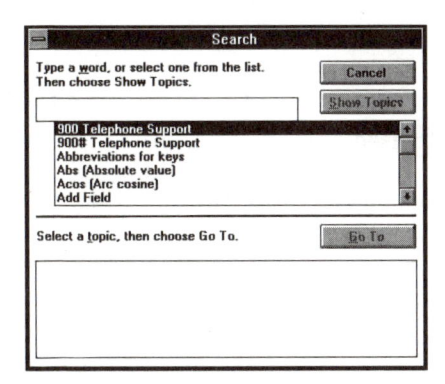

Figure 5.4 The Search dialog box.

2. Type the first few letters of the topic for which you want to search. The list below the text box jumps to the topics that begin with those letters.

3. Double-click on the topic you want from the list, or click once on it and click the Show Topics button. A list of available help screens appears in the lower pane.

4. Double-click on an item in the lower pane, or click on it and click the Go To button. Help for the topic you've chosen appears in the Help window.

5. When you're done reading, double-click the Help window's Control-menu box to close the window and return to Approach.

Other Kinds of Menu Help

In addition to the Contents and the Help Search options, there are many other useful features on the Help menu. Each of those features is summarized below:

Using Help   Provides information about how the Help system works.

For Upgraders   Provides help for users upgrading from the previous version of Approach.

How Do I?   Gives specific instructions for commonly performed tasks.

Keyboard   Shows the various keyboard shortcuts you can use in Approach.

Functions   Provides help with Approach's database management functions.

> **Function**   A common formula used to calculate, for example, today's date—or the date 30 days from now.   *Plain English*

Working Together   Provides help for using Approach with other applications in the Lotus SmartSuite, such as Ami Pro and 1-2-3.

Customer Support   Lists the various Customer Support systems offered by Lotus Development for the users of Lotus Approach.

Tutorial   Runs an on-line tutorial program to help users learn the most common tasks.

About Approach   Tells the version number being used, information about the registered user, and the serial number.

In this lesson, you learned about using the Help facilities afforded to you with Lotus Approach 3.0. In the next lesson, you'll learn how to create new databases.

Lesson 6

Approach Views

In this lesson, you'll learn about the different views that Approach provides for your data.

Approach's Many Views

In Lesson 1, you learned that Approach offers you many different views of your data. This is what makes an Approach file more than just an ordinary database file—the extra views. You can view your information in forms, form letters, reports, worksheets, and charts.

All views are organized with *view tabs*—tabs that run across the top of the Approach window. To see a view, just click on its view tab. If there are many views, not all of the tabs may be visible at once. Use the view tab scroll buttons to scroll among them.

Another way to change views is to select the view you want from a menu. To do so, follow these steps:

1. Click the View button on the status bar. A menu of views appears.

2. Click on the view you want from the list (see Figure 6.1).

Approach Views 31

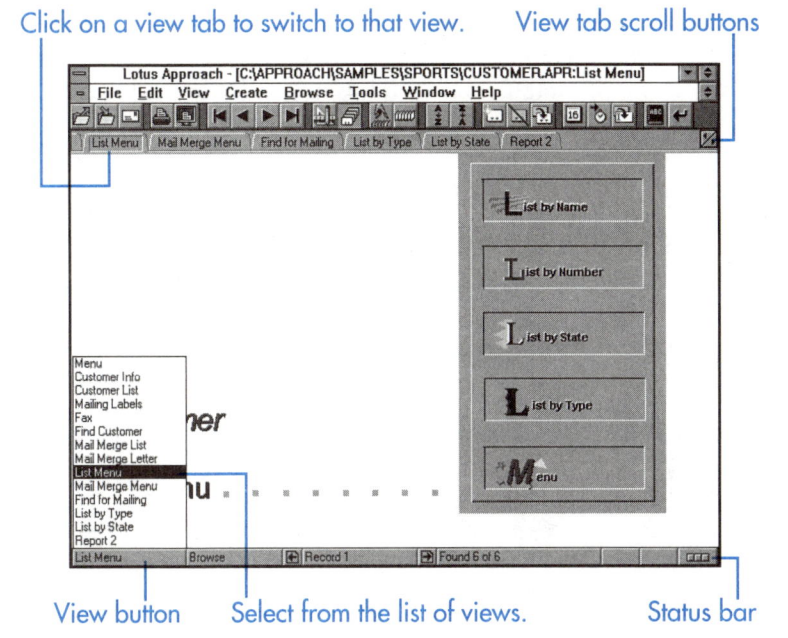

Click on a view tab to switch to that view.   View tab scroll buttons

Figure 6.1   There are several ways to change the view that appears on-screen.

View button   Select from the list of views.   Status bar

> **No Status Bar!**   If you don't see the status bar at the bottom of the screen, select Show Status Bar from Approach's View menu.

The following sections describe the various views you may encounter in Approach. You'll learn more about how to work within each view in later lessons.

Forms View

In Forms view, you view your records one at a time. Each field's data appears in a separate boxed area on the form, as if you were looking at a single paper form that someone had

Lesson 6

filled out for that record. You can page through the records by pressing the PageUp and PageDown keys or by clicking on the right and left arrows at the bottom of the screen (see Figure 6.2).

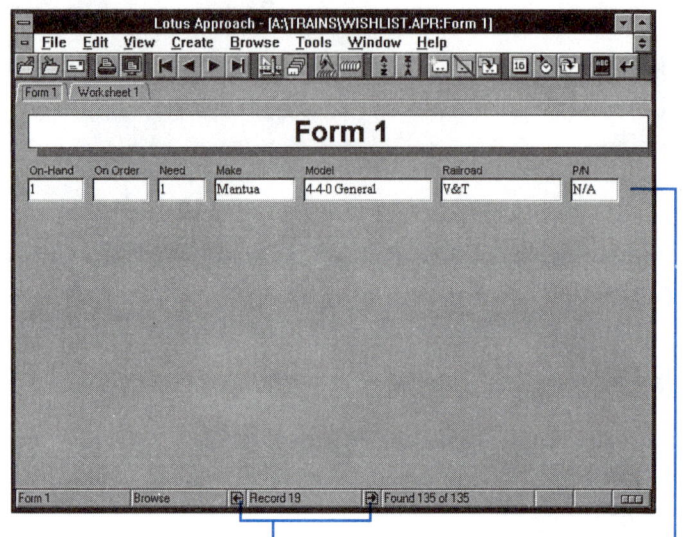

See a different record by clicking on either arrow.

The field entries for one record at a time are displayed.

Figure 6.2 Forms view shows one record at a time.

Approach creates a form automatically when you first open any database. You can see this form at any time by clicking on the tab labelled Form 1.

Worksheet View

Worksheet view is a plain-looking table containing your data. It looks a lot like a spreadsheet might look if you were using it to store data: rows hold individual records, and columns denote the fields. At the intersection of the rows and the columns, the field entries for each record are kept. Figure 6.3 shows a worksheet view. To see the default Worksheet view, click on the Worksheet 1 view tab.

Fields appear as column labels.

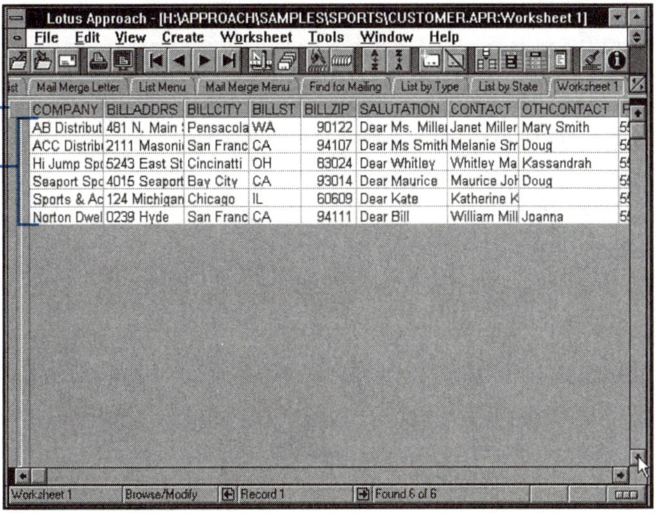
Lotus Approach - [H:\APPROACH\SAMPLES\SPORTS\CUSTOMER.APR:Worksheet 1]
File Edit View Create Worksheet Tools Window Help
Mail Merge Letter
List Menu
Mail Merge Menu
Find for Mailing
List by Type
List by State
Worksheet 1
COMPANY BILLADDRS BILLCITY BILLST BILLZIP SALUTATION CONTACT OTHCONTACT
AB Distribut 481 N. Main Pensacola WA 90122 Dear Ms. Mille Janet Miller Mary Smith
ACC Distrib 2111 Masoni San Franc CA 94107 Dear Ms Smith Melanie Sm Doug
Hi Jump Sp 5243 East St Cincinatti OH 83024 Dear Whitley Whitley Ma Kassandrah
Seaport Spc 4015 Seaport Bay City CA 93014 Dear Maurice Maurice Jol Doug
Sports & Ac 124 Michigan Chicago IL 60609 Dear Kate Katherine K
Norton Dwel 0239 Hyde San Franc CA 94111 Dear Bill William Mill Joanna
Worksheet 1
Browse/Modify
Record 1
Found 6 of 6

Records are displayed in rows.

Figure 6.3 Worksheet view is a plain dump of data. All the records appear in one long list.

Report View

Forms present one record at a time, and worksheets merely present all the records. In contrast, reports enable you to extract meaningful information from the records. For example, let's say you have a database of salespeople that contains 15 fields. If you want to see a list of just the salespeople and their monthly totals, grouped by region, you can design a report to do exactly that. You don't have to wade through the fields or records you don't need to see.

Approach does not create a report automatically (as it does a worksheet and a form), so your database may not have one to view yet. You'll learn to create your own reports in Lesson 13. If there is a report, you can view it by clicking on its view tab. Figure 6.4 shows a report that's been created to summarize Accounts Receivable data.

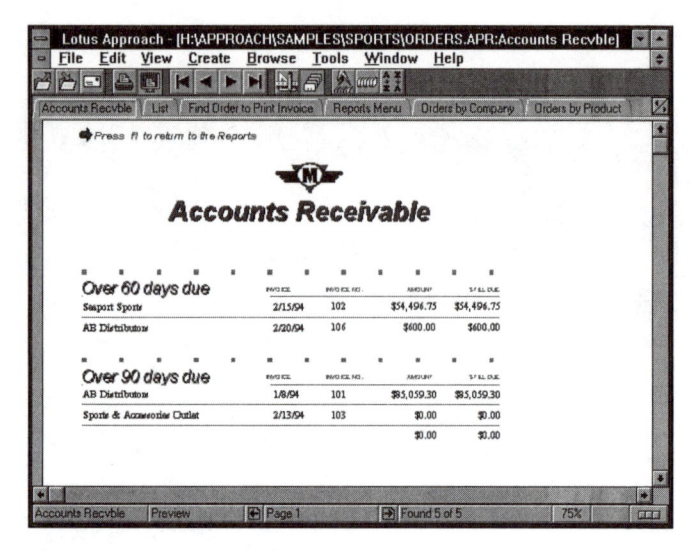

Figure 6.4 A sample report.

Form Letters

Form letters enable you to send the same "personalized" letter to many recipients. The text of the letter does not change, but variable data such as the name and address change so that each person's copy looks as if it were typed specifically for him or her. A sample is shown in Figure 6.5.

You'll learn to create a form letter in Lesson 14. Unlike some other view tabs which are labelled by type (for example, Form 1, Worksheet 2), form letters' view tabs are labelled with the unique name you give them when you create them.

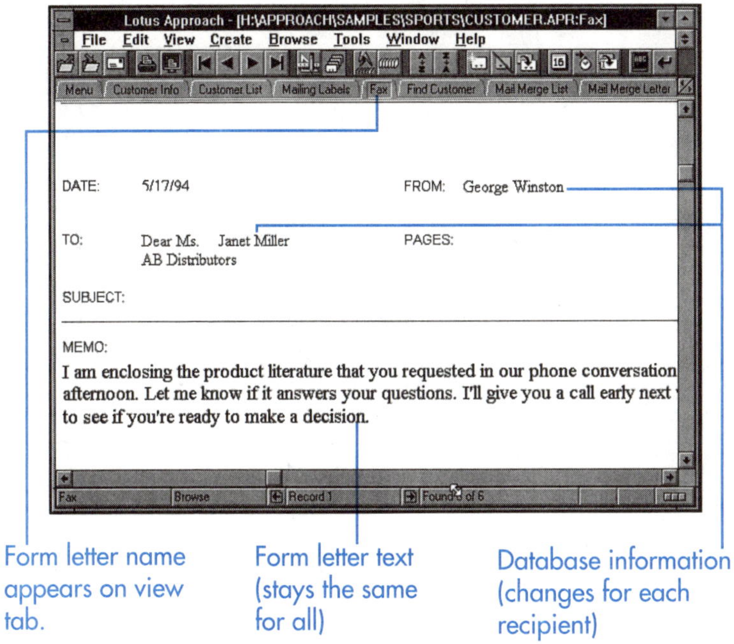
Lotus Approach - [H:\APPROACH\SAMPLES\SPORTS\CUSTOMER.APR:Fax]
File Edit View Create Browse Tools Window Help
Menu
Customer Info
Customer List
Mailing Labels
Fax
Find Customer
Mail Merge List
Mail Merge Letter
DATE: 5/17/94
FROM: George Winston
TO: Dear Ms. Janet Miller
AB Distributors
PAGES:
SUBJECT:
MEMO:
I am enclosing the product literature that you requested in our phone conversation
afternoon. Let me know if it answers your questions. I'll give you a call early next
to see if you're ready to make a decision.
Fax
Browse
Record 1
Form letter name appears on view tab.
Form letter text (stays the same for all)
Database information (changes for each recipient)

Figure 6.5 A sample form letter.

Charts

A chart is a graphical representation of your data. A chart can quickly show the relationships between various values in a way that mere words cannot. (Remember the old saying, "A picture is worth a thousand words?")

You can create four different types of charts: bar, line, area, or pie. You view any of the four types of charts in the same manner that you view any other type of database information: by clicking on its view tab or selecting it from the pop-up menu that appears when you click the View button on the status bar. You'll learn to create a chart in Lesson 15.

Lesson 6

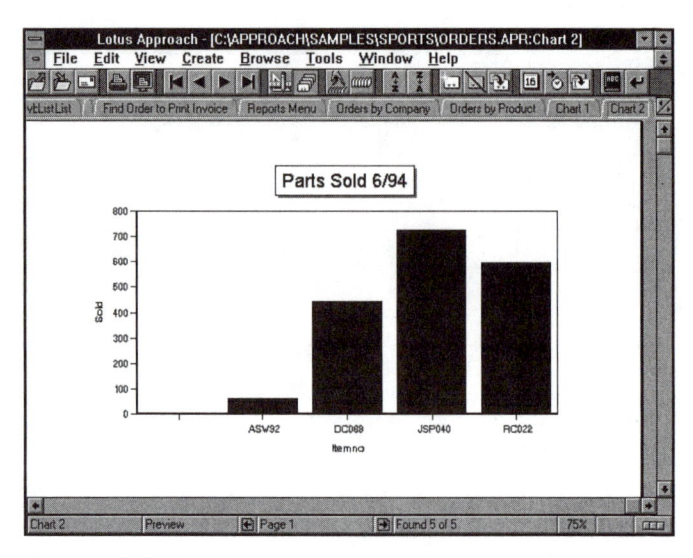

Figure 6.6 A chart shows relationships among data in a graphical way.

What About Modes?

So far we've looked at several views. Some views (such as form view) have two modes: Browse and Design. In Browse mode, you're actually using the view. In Design mode, you're able to make structural changes to the view. You can switch between Browse and Design modes by clicking their SmartIcons or by selecting Browse or Design from the View menu.

Browse SmartIcon

Design SmartIcon

Throughout most of the first part of this book, we'll be working in Browse mode. Later, when we discuss creating your own views, we'll be working in Design mode.

Lesson 7

Creating and Saving a Database

In this lesson, you'll learn to create a new database and save it in an Approach file.

Creating a Database

Unless you already have a database you want to import from another program (as discussed in Lesson 9), your first task in Approach is to create a new database. You have a choice of creating a database from scratch by defining all the fields yourself, or selecting from one of Approach's many *templates*.

> **Template** An Approach template is a predefined set of fields you can use for a specific purpose. For example, the Employees template contains fields you might use to keep track of your employees. Approach comes with over 50 templates.
>
> Plain English

When creating a new Approach database, you first specify the name of the database file you want to create. Then you either define your fields or select a template of fields to use. Follow these steps:

1. Select New from Lotus Approach's File menu. The New dialog box opens.

Lesson 7

2. Type a name for your new database and select a location. Unless you tell Approach otherwise, your new database will be stored in Approach's own directory.

3. Click on the OK button to close the New dialog box and open the Creating New Database dialog box, shown in Figure 7.1.

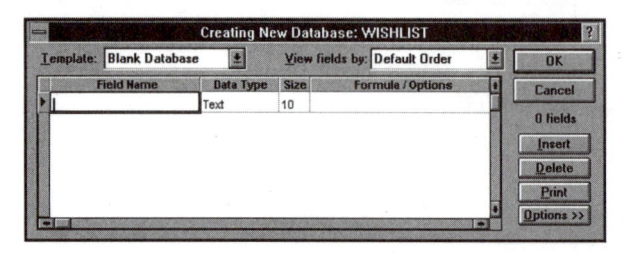

Figure 7.1 The Creating New Database dialog box.

4. If desired, select a template from the Template drop-down list. The fields appear on the field list, and you're done! If you want to create your own fields, select Blank Database from the Template drop-down list and continue with these steps.

5. Enter a name for the field in first empty Field Name blank.

6. Click on the Data Type cell next to the field name you just entered. A down-arrow appears to the right of the blank, indicating that there's a drop-down list available.

7. Open the drop-down list and select a data type.

Creating and Saving a Database 39

What Data Type? There are many data types, but the ones you will use most often are Numeric (for fields that contain only numbers) Text (for fields that contain a mixture of text, symbols, and numbers), and Date (for dates). Approach's on-line help system gives complete details on all the types.

8. Click on the Size cell and type in the maximum number of characters you expect to store in this field. (You can change the size later if necessary.)

9. If you want to add additional fields, click on the empty cell below the field name you just finished defining and repeat steps 5–8 for each additional field.

10. Click on the OK button to save your new Approach file. A form appears on the screen, in which you can add records (you'll learn about adding records in Lesson 10.)

Changing Fields

You can add fields and change the type and size of fields at any time, so don't be in a panic if your new, blank Approach database file doesn't look exactly the way you want it to. If you are using an Approach template, you can also make changes to the field types and sizes in the template's pre-defined fields to customize them for your own use. Here's how:

1. Select Field Definition from the Create menu. The Field Definition dialog box appears (see Figure 7.2).

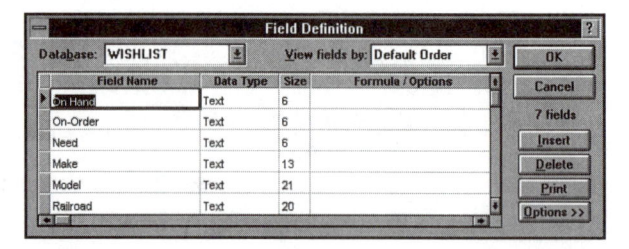

Figure 7.2 The Field Definition dialog box enables you to change the fields in your database.

2. Click on the item you want to change, and type or select a new value.

3. If you want to add a new field, click on the row under the last field name listed, and add the information for the new field.

4. When you're finished, click on OK.

Saving Your Work

Saving your work in Approach is a two-part process—you have already done the first part. When you first create a database, you are asked for the name you want to assign to the database file. That file is the "raw data" file, containing the table of fields and records.

The second part is to save the entire package—the database file plus the Approach views, charts, and so on—as an Approach file. That's what you'll learn in the next section.

Saving an Approach File for the First Time

The first time you save an Approach file, you are asked to name the file. You named the database when you created the fields earlier in this lesson, but now you are naming the

Creating and Saving a Database

Approach file, which consists of not only the database records and fields but also any forms, charts, and so on that you have created.

Here's how you save an Approach file for the first time:

1. Select Save Approach File from the File menu, or click the Save SmartIcon. The Save Approach File dialog box appears.

   > Clicking the Save SmartIcon is the same as selecting Save Approach File from the File menu.

   Where Did That File Name Come From? The name in the File name text box is the name of the database you specified when you began to set up the database. Unless you change it, Approach assumes you want to use the same name for your Approach file.

2. If desired, type a different file name or select a different location for the file.

3. Click OK to accept the file name and location.

   Password Protection To password-protect a file, click on the Set Approach file password check box and type a password in the text box to the right of it. When you reopen the file, Approach will ask for the password again; if you can't remember it, the file won't open!

Your Approach file is now saved, together with all other views and related files. (You haven't created any views or related files yet if you're following along with the tutorial in this book.)

Saving Approach Files—Subsequent Times

Once you've saved an Approach file, you can easily save the changes you make to it. Do any of the following to save changes:

- Select Save Approach File from the File menu.
- Click the Save SmartIcon.
- Press Ctrl+S.

That's it! Approach saves the file with all the same settings that you specified when you first saved the file. To save the file in a different way (for example, with a different name or in a different location), select Save As from the File menu and repeat the procedure for saving for the first time.

Getting Information About a Saved File

Lotus Approach can tell you everything imaginable about your Approach files, from the author's name to the number of fields and records—and everything in between. Follow these steps to see the information available about the Approach file currently on your screen.

1. Select Approach File Info from the File menu. The Approach File Info dialog box opens, as shown in Figure 7.3.

Creating and Saving a Database

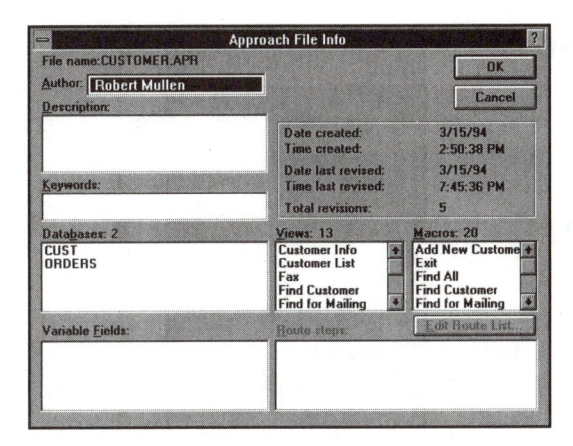

Figure 7.3 The Approach File Info dialog box.

2. Click on the OK button when you are finished looking at the information.

In this lesson, you learned how to create and save Approach files, and how to get information about a saved file. In the next lesson, you'll learn to open Approach files, and how to import data from other programs into Approach.

Lesson 8

Opening Existing Files

In this lesson, you'll learn how to open existing Approach files, and how to import data from other database, spreadsheet, and word processing programs.

When you save a file, you copy it from your computer's memory onto a disk. Conversely, when you open a file, you copy it from the disk to your computer's memory. Approach can open not only its own files, but files from many other programs.

Opening an Approach File

Once you've saved an Approach file to disk, you can reopen it whenever you need to work with it again. Follow these steps to open an Approach file:

1. Select Open from the File menu, or click the Open SmartIcon. The Open dialog box appears.

    Clicking the Open SmartIcon is the same as selecting Open from the File menu.

2. Select the Approach file you want to open. (Change the drive and directory to find the file, if necessary.)

3. Click the OK button. The Approach file appears on your screen for you to work with.

Opening Existing Files 45

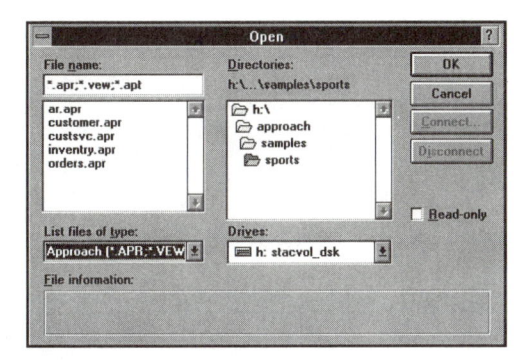

Figure 8.1 The Open dialog box.

If you are opening an Approach file from a previous version of Lotus Approach, after step 3 you'll see a dialog box like the one shown in Figure 8.2. It asks you to confirm that you want to convert the older Approach file to Approach 3.0 format. Click Yes to open the file as an Approach 3.0 file; click No to preserve the old format.

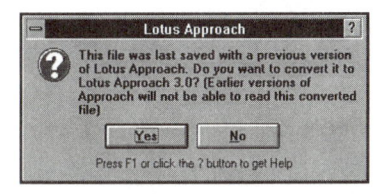

Figure 8.2 The dialog box asking you to confirm the change of format.

Opening Files from Other Database Programs

Approach can also open files from several popular database programs, including dBASE III+ and IV, FoxPro, and Paradox. All you have to do is change the file type in the Open dialog box to show the available files of the type you want. Here's how:

Lesson 8

1. Select Open from the File menu, or click the Open SmartIcon. The Open dialog box appears.

2. Open the List files of type: drop-down list and select the file type you want to open (see Figure 8.3). A list of files created in that program appears in the File name list.

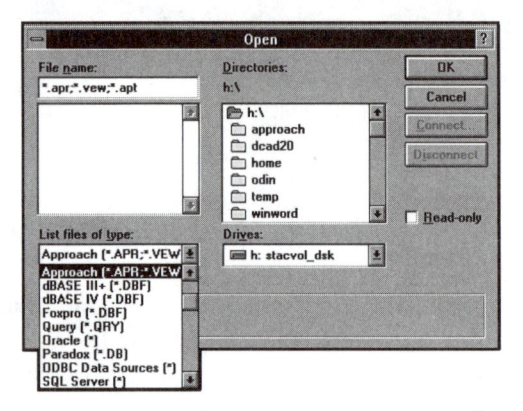

Figure 8.3 Approach can open many types of database files.

3. In the File name list, select the file you want to open. (Change the drive and directory to find the file, if necessary.)

4. Click the OK button. The file is converted to Approach 3.0 format, and it appears on your screen.

> **Back to the Old Format** When you save your work in Approach, you're prompted to save the file as an Approach file, so that the various forms you've created for the data in Approach are preserved. If you want to save the data in its original file format, you'll have to export the information contained in the file. Lesson 9 covers exporting in detail.

Opening Existing Files 47

Opening a Spreadsheet

If you have data stored in a spreadsheet program, you can easily import it into Approach. (Approach can import spreadsheets from Excel or 1-2-3.) When you save the database, the information from the worksheet is saved in Approach's format. The original worksheet stays in its old format; Approach just imported a copy of it.

Create an Approach file from a worksheet with these steps:

1. Select Open from the File menu, or click on the Open SmartIcon.

   Clicking the Open SmartIcon is the same as selecting Open from the File menu.

2. Click on the down-arrow next to the List files of type: box. You'll see a list of file types that Approach can open.

3. Select Excel [*.XLS] or 1-2-3 [*.WK*] depending on the file name extension of the worksheet you want to use.

4. Select the drive, directory, and file name for you worksheet.

5. Click on the OK button. The Field Names dialog box opens (see Figure 8.4).

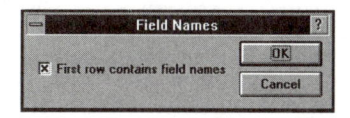

Figure 8.4 You're given a choice between treating the first line of the spreadsheet as field names or as data.

Lesson 8

6. If the first row in the spreadsheet contains data, deselect the First row contains field names check box.

> **My First Row Is a Title!** If the first row of your spreadsheet is anything other than column labels or data, Approach will probably not convert the spreadsheet the way you want it to. Open the spreadsheet in its native program and delete any extra text on the spreadsheet (such as a title or date) before you try to open it in Approach.

7. Click OK to continue.

8. When the Convert To dialog box opens, type a name and select a storage location for your database file.

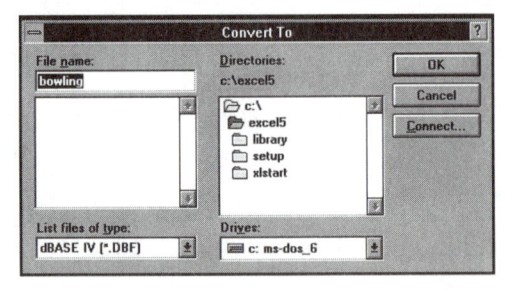

Figure 8.5 The Convert To dialog box looks a lot like the Save dialog box you've already encountered.

9. Click OK. Approach converts the spreadsheet data to a database file.

If you'd like to see the entire database on the screen in a format more similar to the original worksheet, click on the Worksheet 1 view tab. You can switch among any of the views by clicking on the view tabs at any time.

Opening a Text File

You can easily convert data from a text file or word processing program into an Approach file. Just insert tabs or commas between the fields in the text file, and Approach will use those characters to create fields in the Approach file. (Approach interprets paragraph markers—"hard returns"—as end-of-record markers.)

> **Why Would I Use a Text File?** The capability to open a text file and save it as an Approach file is really handy if you're stuck working with another database management software product. If Approach will not import data from the database program you used to create the file, you can export it from that program as a text file, and then import it into Approach as the same.

There are two types of text files from which to choose. *Text-Fixed Length* enables you to easily use text information that's already arranged in columns in the existing text file. With the *Text-Delimited* file type, you tell Approach if it's okay to use special characters (like tabs or commas) that exist in the text file to organize the Approach file you're creating. Text-Delimited is the more commonly used type, since few text files include real columns.

In this example, we'll import a text-delimited file into Approach:

1. Select Open from the File menu, or click on the Open SmartIcon. The Open dialog box appears.

2. Click on the down-arrow next to the List files of type: list box to see the file formats available. Select Text-Delimited (for this example).

3. Type a file name and select a location. Then click on the OK button. The Text File Options dialog box opens, as shown in Figure 8.6.

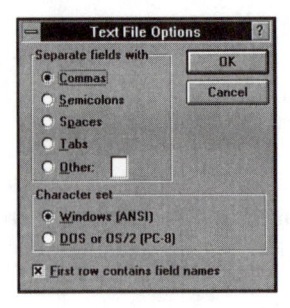

Figure 8.6 The Text File Options dialog box.

4. Based on how the text is separated in your text file, click on one of the option buttons in the Separate fields with: group box. For example, if your text file has commas separating text types, click on the Commas option box.

5. By default, Approach uses the text in the first record (on the first line) as the field names. (It figures you have column labels there.) If your first line is an actual record, deselect the First row contains field names check box now.

> **Title on the First Line?** Just like with spreadsheets, if the first line of your text file is anything other than column labels or data, Approach will probably not convert the data correctly. Open the text file in its native program and delete all the text except the data and the column labels before you try to open it in Approach.

6. Click on the OK button. You'll be asked to name your new database file.

7. Type a name and select a location, and then click on the OK button. Approach converts the information in your text file into a new database file.

Approach displays the results of the text conversion in Forms view. Click on the Worksheet 1 view tab to see your database displayed in rows and columns, if you prefer.

In this lesson, you learned to open files—Approach files, other database program files, spreadsheets, and text files. In the next lesson, you'll learn about importing and exporting data.

Lesson 9

Importing and Exporting Information

In this lesson, you'll learn how to import your data to and export data from other programs.

Why Import and Export?

While Approach enables you to open and close files created with other applications as simply as if they were all Approach files, the Import/Export process allows you to *add* information to an existing Approach database. In this way, you can combine the information of several databases in any of the supported file formats to create one larger, more comprehensive database.

Even though you can open foreign-format files directly into Approach, you cannot save Approach files directly into foreign formats. If you need to save your data in a format other than Approach's own, you must *export* it.

Importing Data

In Approach, you can add the information from a supported database file format into an existing Approach file. However, to do so you must open the Approach file you want to add to, and then import the data. For example, if you had two customer databases, one in Approach and one in dBASE IV, you could import the dBASE IV database into the Approach database to create a single database.

Importing and Exporting Information 53

Importing from a Database File

Here's how you import information from a database file into an existing Approach file:

1. Open the Approach file that will receive the imported data.

2. Select Import Data from Approach's File menu. The Import Data dialog box opens.

3. Select the database that you want to import, and then click on the OK button. The Import Setup dialog box opens, as shown in Figure 9.1. The Data from list shows the fields in the database being imported. The Fields in list shows the fields in your selected Approach database.

Fields in the database being imported

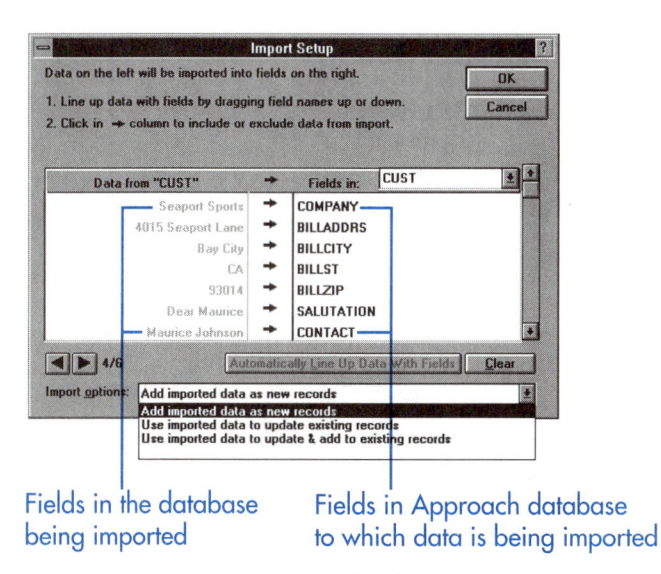

Fields in Approach database to which data is being imported

Figure 9.1 The Import Setup dialog box.

4. Make sure the correct database is shown next to Fields in:. If not, select it from the drop-down list.

5. Drag the fields on the right (the ones under Fields in) up or down until they line up with the corresponding grayed-out field names (under Data from) to your satisfaction.

> **Auto-Align** Instead of dragging in step 5, you can click on the Automatically Line Up Data With Fields button to have Approach find matches based on field name. Click on the Clear button to start this matching process over if you need to.

6. If desired, click on the right and left arrow buttons in the bottom left corner of the dialog box to view actual data in the database to be imported. (It sometimes helps to see actual data when matching fields.)

7. Open the Import options drop-down list and select a method for importing the data. You are given the following choices:

   - Add imported data as new records: Adds imported records as new records at the end of your database.

   - Use imported data to update existing records: Updates existing data in your database.

   - Use imported data to update & add to existing records: Updates matching records in your existing database and adds all non-matching data as new records.

8. Click on the OK button to import the data.

Your Approach file now includes the data that you imported from another database file of a supported format. Note the expanded record count in your Approach file once you've completed the import process. It should reflect the sum total of both the recipient and imported databases, unless you opted to update existing records in your Approach database.

> **Original's Still There** Importing information does not affect the original file being imported in any way. It will still exist in the other program, with information completely intact, after you've imported its data!

Importing Spreadsheet Data

Importing data from a spreadsheet file is much the same as importing data from a database (as described in the previous section). The only difference is that when you select the spreadsheet file to import, an additional dialog box appears, as shown in Figure 9.2.

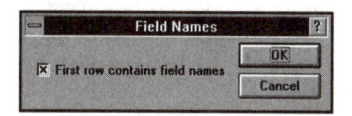

Figure 9.2 The Field Names dialog box.

If the first row in your spreadsheet contains field names, leave this check box selected. If the first row contains an actual record, deselect the check box. When you're done, click OK and continue importing exactly as you would with a database file.

Exporting Information

If you want to extract information from Approach into a format that another program can use, you must export it. When you export from Approach, you export the data only—not any of the views. Here's how you export information from an Approach file:

Lesson 9

1. Open the Approach file that contains the data you want to export.

2. Select Export Data from Approach's File menu. The Export Data dialog box opens (see Figure 9.3).

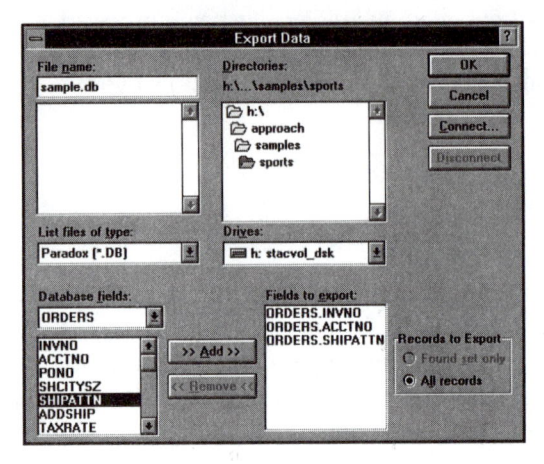

Figure 9.3 The Export Data dialog box.

3. Select a data type from the List files of type: list.

4. Select the file that will receive the exported data, or type a new file name if you want to create a new file to hold it.

5. Select the fields to export from the Database fields list box. Click on the >>Add>> button to move the fields into the Fields to Export list.

6. Click on the OK button. The Choose Key Field dialog box opens (Figure 9.4).

7. Click on the field that you wish to use as the key or index field. Then click on the OK button to complete the Export process.

   The information in your Approach file is exported into an "alien" file in the format that you chose.

Importing and Exporting Information

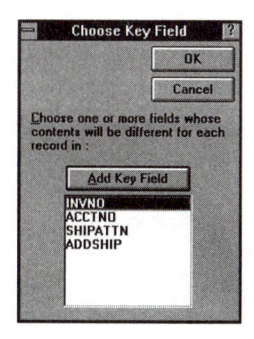

Figure 9.4 The Choose Key Field dialog box.

Exporting for Your Word Processor

Lots of people export database information into text so that they can use their word processor to spell check the contents of their database. They then reopen the text file as an Approach file using the steps in Lesson 8 for opening a text file.

Exporting to a text file is the same as exporting to any other format, except that you are asked to specify a delimiter character. A *delimiter character* is the character to be placed between fields to mark them. The most commonly used delimiters are commas and tabs.

Here's how to export to a text file:

1. Open the Approach or database file.

2. Select Export Data from Approach's File menu. The Export Data dialog box will open (see Figure 9.3).

3. Select Text Delimited - [*.TXT] from the List files of type: list.

4. Type a name for your text file in the File name box.

5. Select the fields you want to export from the Database fields: list. Then click the >>Add>> button to move them to the Fields to export: list.

Lesson 9

6. Click on the OK button.

7. Choose the appropriate delimiter in the Text File Options dialog box (shown in Figure 9.5), and then click on the OK button.

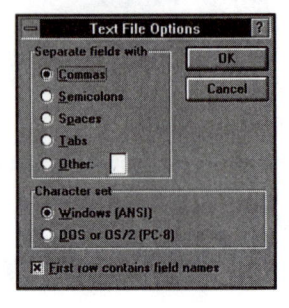

Figure 9.5 The Text File Options dialog box enables you to select a delimiter character.

Which Delimiter Character? Choose the character to use for delimiting based on the capabilities of your word processor or other application that's destined to use that text file. If you retain the delimiting characters in your text file, you can easily import that file back into an Approach database!

Approach places a copy of your selected database into a new text file, delimited with the characters you opted for in the Text File Options dialog box.

In this lesson, you learned how to import and export data with Approach, for exchange with other applications. In the next lesson, you'll learn how to add records to a database.

Lesson 10

Adding Records to a Database

In this lesson, you'll learn how to add records to an open database.

If you're reading this book lesson by lesson, you now have an empty shell of a database that you created in Lesson 7, or you have an imported database that you opened in Lesson 8 or 9. In this lesson, you'll add some records to that database.

In this lesson and in Lessons 11 and 12, we'll be working in Browse mode in Forms view. If you are following the lessons in order, you are already in Browse mode and Forms view. If you have any doubts, follow these steps to switch to them now:

1. Click on the Browse SmartIcon (see Figure 10.1).

2. Click on the Form 1 view tab or another tab that represents a form.

In the examples in the next few lessons, we are using the ORDERS database that comes with Approach, and we're using a form called Order.

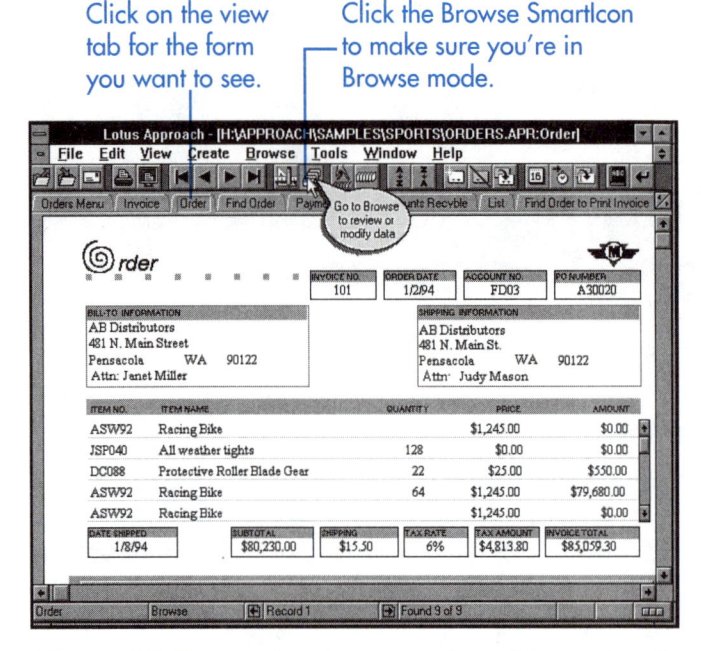

Figure 10.1 Switch to Browse mode and Forms view if you're not already there.

Adding New Records

You can add records in either Forms view or Worksheet view, but you will probably find Forms view the easiest to use, since it shows only one record at a time. Here's how you add a new record using Forms view:

1. Select New Record from the Browse menu, or press Ctrl+N, or click on the New Record SmartIcon. All the fields on the form are wiped clean, leaving them ready for your new data (see Figure 10.2).

   Clicking on the New Record SmartIcon is the same as selecting New Record from the Browse menu or pressing Ctrl+N.

Adding Records to a Database

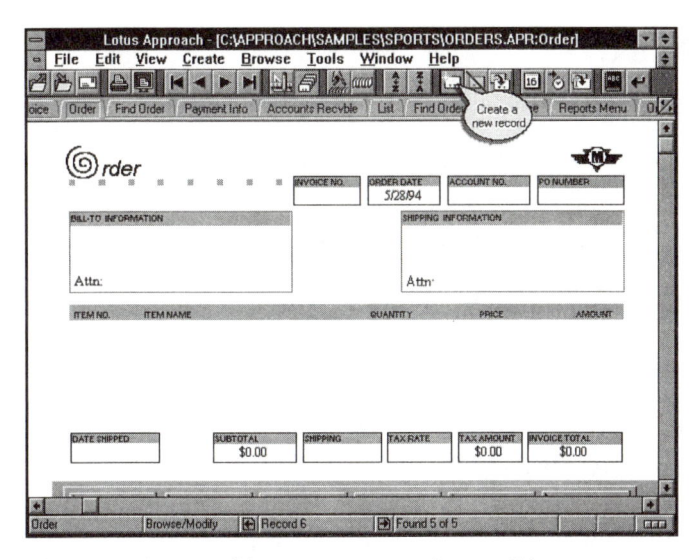

Figure 10.2 Adding a new record. (You'll learn to create a fancy form like this one later.)

2. Click in the first field on the form and type that field's entry for this record.

3. Press Tab to move to the next field, or click in the next field.

4. Continue typing field entries and moving to the next field until all fields have been completed for this record. You can skip a field if it is not applicable.

5. To enter another record, click again on the New Record SmartIcon. Follow these steps for each record, until you've entered all your records.

In this lesson, you learned to add records to a database. In the next lesson, you'll learn to find, edit, and delete records.

Lesson 11

Finding, Editing, and Deleting Records

In this lesson, you'll learn how to search a database to locate a specific record. Once you find it, you'll learn to edit or delete it.

One thing is for certain: database files are never completely up to date. Something always has to be changed or deleted. Before you can edit or delete a record, however, you must find it.

Finding Records

At first, finding records might seem easy: you just browse through until you find the one you want. But when your number of records grows to 100 or even 1000, it becomes very difficult to find the record you want simply by browsing through.

> If you're in Design mode, you need to switch back to Browse mode before you can edit a record. Click on the Browse SmartIcon to make sure you're in Browse mode if you have any doubts.

1. If it's not already open on your screen, click the tab for the form you want to use (for example, Form 1).

Finding, Editing, and Deleting Records   63

2. Select Find from the Browse menu, or press Ctrl+F, or click on the Find SmartIcon. The fields on the form are emptied, and the Find bar appears between the form and the icon bar (see Figure 11.1).

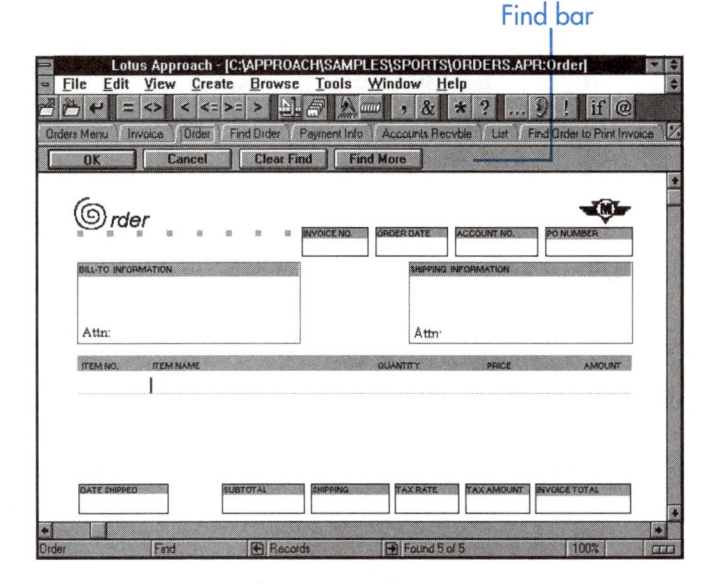

Figure 11.1 Finding a record.

> Clicking on the Find SmartIcon is the same as selecting Find from the Browse menu or pressing Ctrl+F.

3. In the field that you want to search, type text that matches the entry for the record you want to find. For example, if you want to find the record with the invoice number 101, type 101 in the INVOICE NO. field.

Lesson 11

> **Placement Is Important!** Make sure you type your information in the same field in which it appears in the record. If you type text in the wrong field, Approach will report that the information is not found.

4. Click on the OK button on the Find bar or press Enter. The record you seek appears on-screen.

> **Record Not Found** If Approach can't find any records that match the text you typed, it will display a dialog box with an error message to that effect. Try again!

Should Approach find multiple records that match the text you entered, only the first one will appear on-screen in step 4. You can see the others by pressing PageUp or PageDown, or by clicking on the arrow buttons on the status bar. The status bar will report the number of matching records found (see Figure 11.2).

Click here to see other matching records.

| Order | Browse | Record 1 | Found 9 of 9 |

Records found during the Find operation

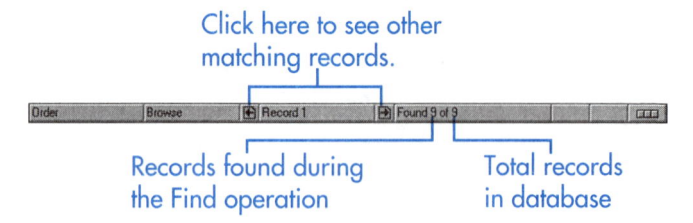

Total records in database

Figure 11.2 The status bar reports the number of matching records found.

Finding Multiple Records

In trying to find a single record, you may have accidentally found multiple records. You can also find multiple records on purpose; in fact, Approach has special commands that make it easy for you to find many records at once.

Notice that when you select the Find command, the SmartIcon palette changes, offering SmartIcons specific to finding records. Table 9.1 shows the ones that are different from the regular SmartIcon palette.

Table 9.1 SmartIcons for Finding Records.

SmartIcon	Function
=	Finds items equal to
<>	Finds items not equal to
<	Finds items less than
<=	Finds items less than or equal to
>=	Finds items greater than or equal to
>	Finds items greater than
,	Finds items that match either criteria
&	Finds items that match both criteria
*	Finds any string
?	Finds any character
...	Finds items with a range
👂	Finds items that sound like
!	Finds items with case sensitivity

continues

Table 9.1 Continued

SmartIcon	Function
if	Finds items when expression is true
@	Prefaces Approach functions in the search string

You can use any combination of these symbols to specify a subset of the records that you want to find. Place the symbols in the field you are searching by placing the cursor in the appropriate field and clicking on the appropriate button. For example, in the sample ORDERS database that comes with Approach, we want to find all records that have an order date of 1/2/94 and have ordered either item number ASW92 or any item whose item number begins with J. Follow these steps:

1. Select Find from the Browse menu, or click the Find SmartIcon.

2. Type 2/1/94 in the Order Date field.

3. Click on the item name field.

4. Type J*. This signifies that you want to find "anything beginning with J."

5. Click the OK button on the Find bar or press Enter. Approach finds the specified records.

A full explanation of all the available Find SmartIcons is beyond the scope of this book. Experiment with them or see your Approach documentation for more details.

Finding, Editing, and Deleting Records   67

Changing Records

Periodically you may need to change the information in one or more fields in a record. Approach makes it very easy to do. Just find the record, display it on-screen, and make your changes.

1. Find the record (using the Find procedure you just learned).

2. Move to the field you want to change and backspace over the old information.

3. Type the revised data for that field.

Deleting Records

Some records may become outdated and useless. When this happens, you will want to delete them to avoid clutter in your database. Here's how:

1. Find the record you want to delete (using the Find procedure you learned earlier in this lesson) and display it on-screen.

> **Decisions, Decisions!** If Approach finds more than one record that matches your criteria, use the PageUp and PageDown keys to scroll through the matching records until you locate the *exact* record you wish to delete. Don't just delete the first one you see!

2. Select Delete Record from the Browse menu, or press Ctrl+Delete, or click on the Delete SmartIcon.

> Clicking on the Delete SmartIcon is the same as selecting Delete Record from the Browse menu or pressing Ctrl+Delete.

3. When Approach asks you to confirm that you want to permanently delete the selected record, click on the Yes button to do so.

Deleting Several Records

You can also delete many records at once. Follow these steps:

1. Find the group of records you want to delete using the Find command.

2. Select Delete Found Set from the Browse menu.

3. When Approach asks you to confirm that you want to delete the selected records, click on the Yes button.

In this lesson, you learned how to add, find, change, and delete records. In the next lesson, you'll learn how to sort and retrieve information.

Lesson 12

Sorting Your Records

In this lesson, you'll learn how to sort the records in your database.

Approach's Powerful Sorting Capabilities

Lotus Approach wouldn't be a powerful database management tool without strong information-sorting capabilities. You can sort your data by any field, in either ascending or descending alphabetical order. Figure 12.1 shows you a database that is sorted in ascending order according to the Item no. field. Figure 12.2 shows the same database sorted with descending item numbers.

Ascending and Descending When ascending order is used, your records are listed from lowest to highest (from 0–100 and then A–Z, for example). When descending order is used, your database records are arranged from highest to lowest (from Z–A and then 100–0).

Plain English

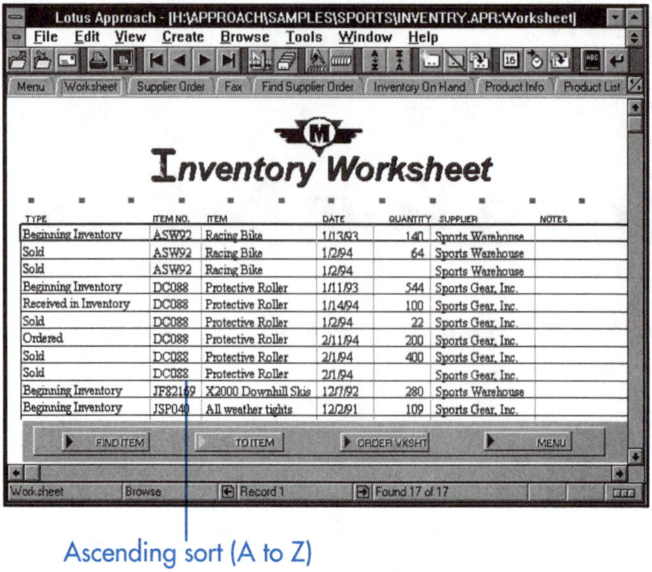

Figure 12.1 These records are sorted in ascending order.

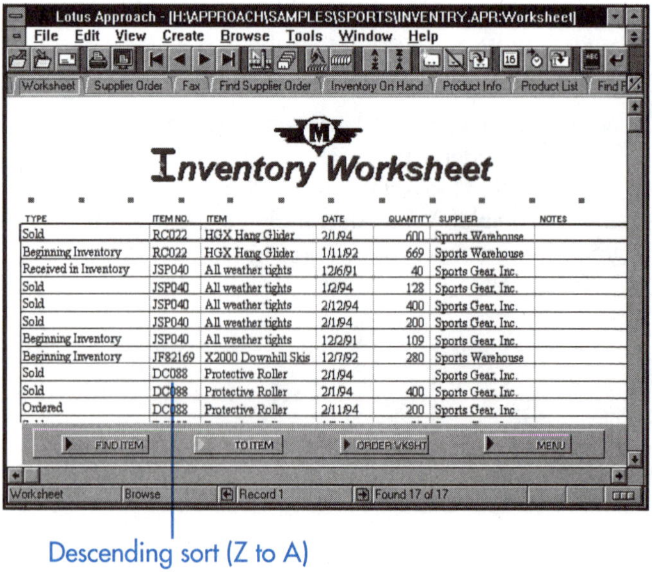

Figure 12.2 These records are sorted in descending order.

Sorting in Form View

Even though you can see only one record at a time in Form view, you can still sort the entire database by a particular field. Follow these steps:

1. In Form view, click on the field by which you want to sort. An insertion point appears at the end of the entry in that field.

2. Click on the Ascending Sort or Descending Sort SmartIcon, or select Sort from the Browse menu and then select Ascending or Descending.

    For example, if you wanted to sort your database from A to Z by the Item field, you would click on the entry in the Item field on the form, and then click the Ascending Sort SmartIcon.

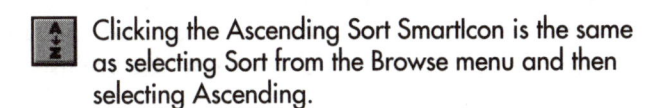

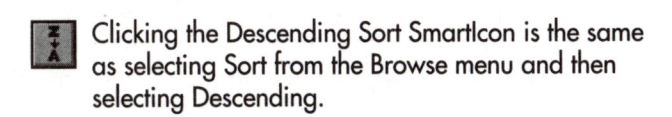

> Clicking the Ascending Sort SmartIcon is the same as selecting Sort from the Browse menu and then selecting Ascending.

> Clicking the Descending Sort SmartIcon is the same as selecting Sort from the Browse menu and then selecting Descending.

Sorting in Worksheet View

Many people prefer to sort in Worksheet view because they can see the results of their sort immediately, since Worksheet view shows many records on-screen at once. To sort in Worksheet view, follow these steps.

1. In Worksheet view, click on the field name (the column label) for the field on which you want to sort. The entire column appears highlighted.

The Column Isn't Highlighted! If you're working with the sample database that comes with Approach, be aware that the worksheets, forms, and reports in this database have been fancied up to the point where they don't work exactly like a "plain" database that you create yourself. If you click on a column heading and nothing happens, just click on any field under the desired column. Your sort will still work fine.

2. Click the Ascending Sort or Descending Sort SmartIcon, or select Sort from the Worksheet menu and then select Ascending or Descending.

Notice that when you're in Forms view, there is a Browse menu, but when you switch to Worksheet view, it changes to a Worksheet menu. That's because the commands you use in Forms view are very different from those available in Worksheet view. The Sort command appears on whichever menu is applicable to the view you are using.

Custom Sorting

Sometimes a simple ascending or descending sort is not enough. You may need to sort by several fields at once, for instance. Follow these steps to perform more advanced sorts:

1. Select Sort from Approach's Browse menu and select Define. The Sort dialog box opens, as shown in Figure 12.3.

2. The first field in the database may appear on the Fields to sort on: list. If it does and you want to use it as your primary sort field, click on it. Then click the Ascending or Descending button to specify the sort order.

Sorting Your Records   73

Database text box   Fields on which to sort

[Sort dialog box image with Database fields list on left showing INVENTRY, RECEIVED, SOLD, INVNO, DATE, NOTES, AMTORDER, DATEORD, SUBJECT; Fields to sort on showing INVENTRY.ITEMNO; Add, Remove, Clear All buttons; OK, Cancel, Ascending, Descending, Summaries buttons]

Database fields list

Figure 12.3 The Sort dialog box.

  3. If you don't want to use the field that appears on the Fields to sort on: list as your primary sort field, click on it and click the <<Remove<< button.

  4. If you want to sort by another field, click on it on the Database fields: list and click the >>Add>> button to add it to the Fields to sort on: list. Click the Ascending or Descending button as desired for that field.

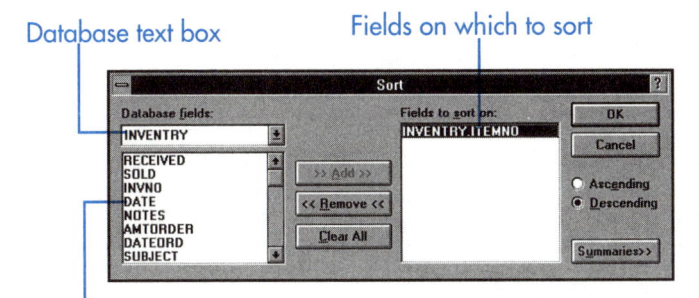

  5. Repeat step 4 until you have specified all the fields you want to sort by, in the order you want to sort them.

  6. Click on the OK button to sort your records.

For instance, if you select DATE, CUSTOMER, and TOTALAMT (in that order) as your sort fields, Approach will sort the entire database by date. If there are records that have the same date, it will sort them by customer. If there are any records that have the same date and customer name, Approach will sort them by the total amount.

In this lesson, you learned how to sort records. In the next lesson, you'll learn how to work with numbers stored in your database files.

Lesson 13

Creating Reports and Worksheets

In this lesson, you'll learn to create a report from your Approach data, and to create additional worksheets.

Creating a Report

You learned about reports earlier in this book, and you've seen how they can extract the most important information from your database and present it in an easy-to-read format. The old days of green-shaded fan-fold printer paper are gone forever. Your printed reports will look as slick as the professionally prepared printed matter that was previously distributed only to upper management and stockholders.

Approach provides a Report Assistant that walks you through the process of creating a report, making it as painless as possible. Here's how you create a report with the Report Assistant:

1. Open the Approach file or database from which you want to create a report.

2. Select Report from Approach's Create menu. The Report Assistant dialog box opens.

3. In the View name & title: text box, type a name for your new report.

4. Open the SmartMaster style: drop-down list and select a color and style combination.

Creating Reports and Worksheets   75

Color and Style?   For best results, choose B&W selections unless you have a color printer.

5. Click on a layout listed in the SmartMaster layout list, and an example of what it will look like appears in the Sample Report area (see Figure 13.1). Click on various layout names until you find the one you want.

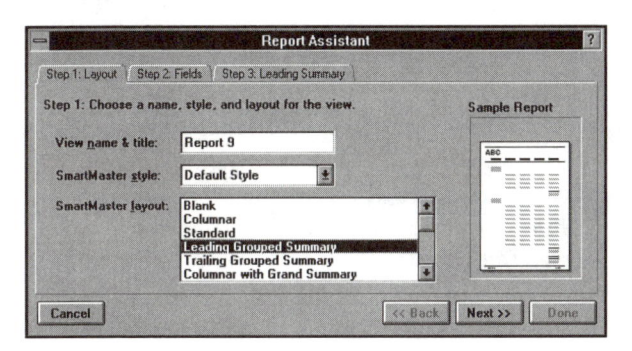

Figure 13.1   The Report Assistant dialog box.

6. Click the Next>> button to continue. The dialog box changes to the one shown in Figure 13.2.

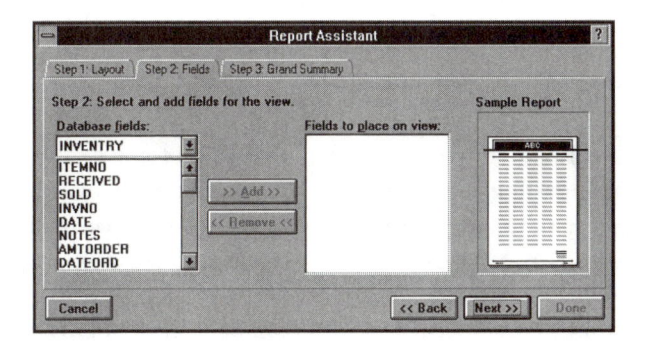

Figure 13.2   The second phase of the Report Assistant dialog box.

7. Make sure the database for which you want to create the report appears in the Database fields box. If not, open the drop-down list and select it.

8. Under Database fields:, click on the field names that you want to include in the report, and then click the >>Add>> button to move them to the Fields to place on view: list.

9. If there is a tab for a third step on the dialog box, the >>Next>> button will appear in the lower right corner of the dialog box. If so, click on it to continue. If not, click Done to close the dialog box.

> **Why a Third Step?** Some reports require a third step; others do not. Skip step 10 if you selected Done in step 9.

10. If there is a third step for creating your report, follow the instructions on-screen to complete it. Then click Done to close the dialog box.

Congratulations! You've just used Report Assistant to create your first report. Don't forget to save your Approach file before you go on.

Customizing a Report

You can customize your report in a variety of ways: you can move the headings around and resize them, rearrange the order of the data, add graphics, and more. The procedures for customizing a report are very similar to customizing any other view. You access Design mode by clicking the Design SmartIcon or by selecting Design from the View menu. From there, you drag objects around or double-click on them to edit them.

Creating Reports and Worksheets 77

For more complete help using Design mode to customize a report, see Lessons 17 and 18.

Creating Additional Worksheets

When you create a new database, Approach automatically creates a worksheet and a form. As time goes by, however, you may want additional worksheets. (Creating additional forms is covered later in this book.)

The advantage of having an additional worksheet is that you can choose which fields appear on it—you need not include all the fields. If you have many fields that you seldom refer to, you may want to eliminate them to create a worksheet that includes only the fields you most often need to see.

Here's how you create a worksheet:

1. Open the Approach file or database for which you want to create the extra worksheet.

2. Select Worksheet from the Create menu. The Worksheet Assistant dialog box opens (see Figure 13.3).

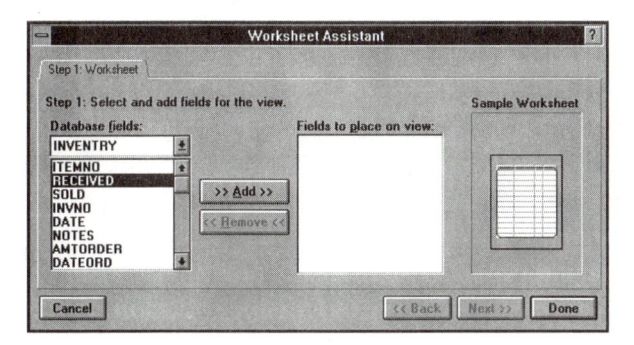

Figure 13.3 The Worksheet Assistant dialog box.

3. Select the fields you want to include from the Database fields: list, and click the >>Add>> button to add them to the new worksheet.

4. Click Done to create the new worksheet.

You'll now see a worksheet on your screen. Figure 13.4 shows you a sample worksheet created with Worksheet Assistant.

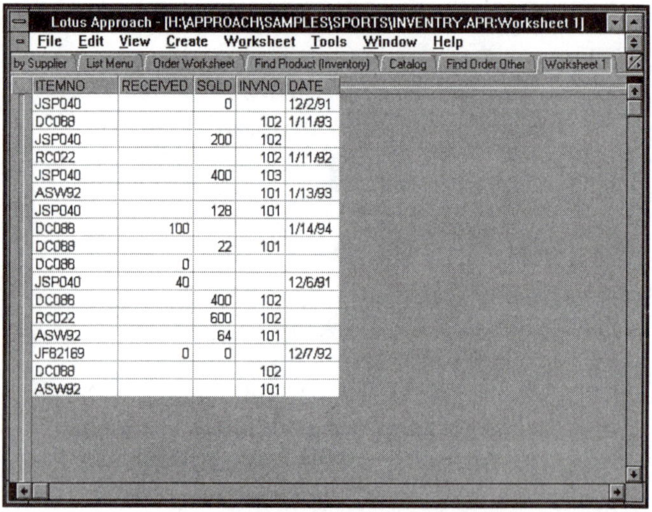

ITEMNO	RECEIVED	SOLD	INVNO	DATE
JSP040		0		12/2/91
DC088			102	1/11/93
JSP040		200	102	
RC022			102	1/11/92
JSP040		400	103	
ASW92			101	1/13/93
JSP040		128	101	
DC088	100			1/14/94
DC088		22	101	
DC088	0			
JSP040	40			12/6/91
DC088		400	102	
RC022		600	102	
ASW92		64	101	
JFB2169	0	0		12/7/92
DC088			102	
ASW92			101	

Figure 13.4 A worksheet created with Worksheet Assistant.

Your new worksheet will have its own view tab named Worksheet1. You can click on it to see your worksheet any time you want to.

In this lesson, you learned to create a new report or worksheet. In the next lesson, you'll learn to create mailing labels and form letters.

Lesson 14

Mailing Labels and Form Letters

In this lesson, you'll learn to create mailing labels and form letters from an Approach database file.

Mailing labels and form letters are two variations on the same theme: sending mass mailings with each item personalized for the recipient. Mailing labels and form letters often go together; the form letter goes on the inside of the envelope and the mailing label on the outside. In this lesson you'll learn to create both.

> **No Names and Addresses in Your Database?** You'll want to use a database that contains names and addresses for these steps; otherwise you may get strange results! You can create one for this purpose or use one of the sample databases that come with Approach (such as Customer) that contains names and addresses.

Making Mailing Labels

Lotus Approach helps you get your mail to the right place with no mistakes in addressing. Approach will create and print mailing labels from the information in any Approach file or database.

Here's how you create mailing labels with Lotus Approach:

1. Open an Approach database or file that contains addresses.

2. Select Mailing Label from the Create menu. The Mailing Label Assistant dialog box opens, as shown in Figure 14.1.

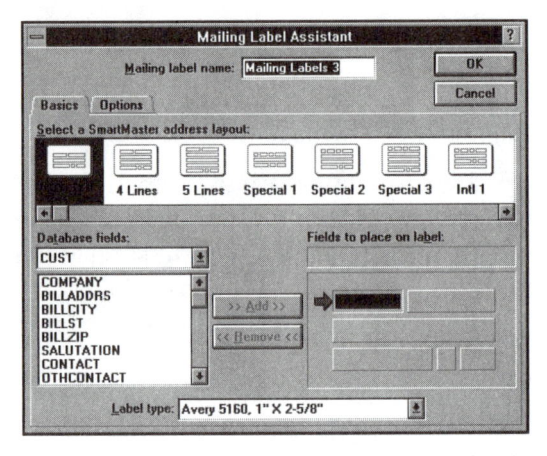

Figure 14.1 The Mailing Label Assistant dialog box.

3. Type a name for your label in the Mailing label name box.

4. Select a SmartMaster address label layout by clicking on a layout picture. (Use the scroll bar to see more layout choices.)

5. Click on a field on the Database fields list.

6. In the bottom right corner of the dialog box is a diagram of gray rectangles representing positions on the label. Click on a rectangle and click the >>Add button to place the selected field in it.

Mailing Labels and Form Letters 81

7. Repeat steps 5-6 until you have assigned a field to every gray rectangle, or until you have assigned all the fields you want to use.

8. Click on the Label Type drop-down list and select the type of labels on which you will be printing.

9. Select OK. Approach creates your mailing labels, (see Figure 14.2).

Figure 14.2 shows you mailing labels that I created in just a minute or two—on my first try!

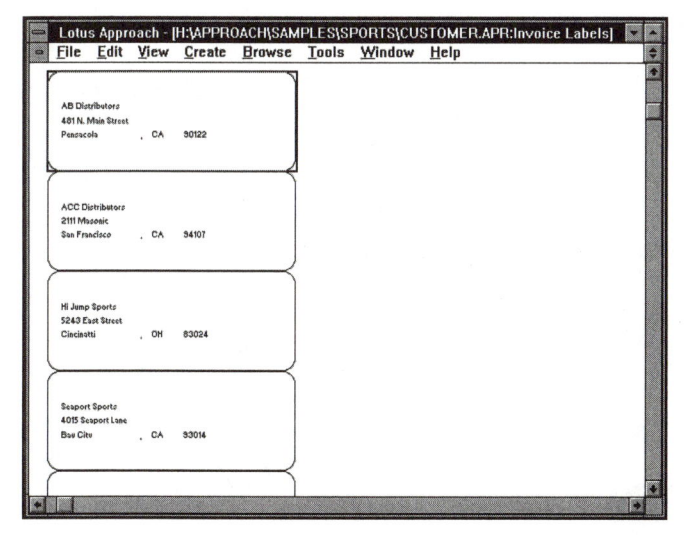

```
Lotus Approach - [H:\APPROACH\SAMPLES\SPORTS\CUSTOMER.APR:Invoice Labels]
File  Edit  View  Create  Browse  Tools  Window  Help

AB Distributors
401 N. Main Street
Pensacola        , CA   90122


ACC Distributors
2111 Masonic
San Francisco    , CA   94107


Hi Jump Sports
5243 East Street
Cincinatti       , OH   83024


Seaport Sports
4015 Seaport Lane
Bas City         , CA   83014
```

Figure 14.2 Mailing labels created with Mailing Label Assistant.

> **Save Me!** Don't forget to save your work. Just save your Approach file in order to save everything you've just created.

You print mailing labels just like you print any other form; see Lesson 21 for details.

Creating a Form Letter

Approach enables you to compose a letter to several recipients and use the data from your database file to personalize the letter for each one. Follow these steps as you work through the multi-step process with Approach's Form Letter Assistant.

1. Open the Approach or database file that contains the names and addresses of the recipients.

2. Select Form Letter from the Create menu. The Form Letter Assistant dialog box opens, as shown in Figure 14.3.

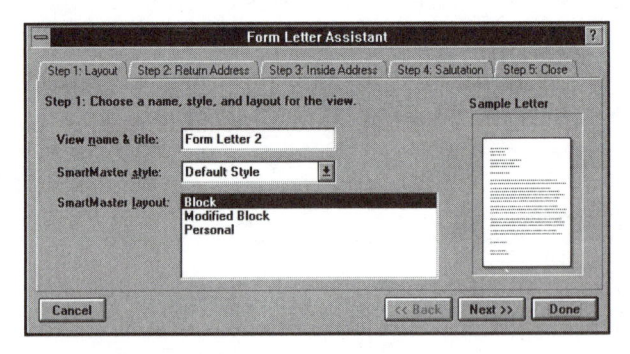

Figure 14.3 The Form Letter Assistant dialog box.

3. Type a name for the form letter in the View name & title text box.

4. Open the SmartMaster layout drop-down list and select a layout.

5. Choose a SmartMaster style from the style list.

6. Click on the Next >> button to continue. The controls for Step 2 of this process appear.

7. Select the None radio button to omit the return address (for instance, if you use letterhead

Mailing Labels and Form Letters

stationery), or type a return address in the text box provided.

8. Click on the Next >> button to continue. The controls for Step 3 of the process appear (see Figure 14.4).

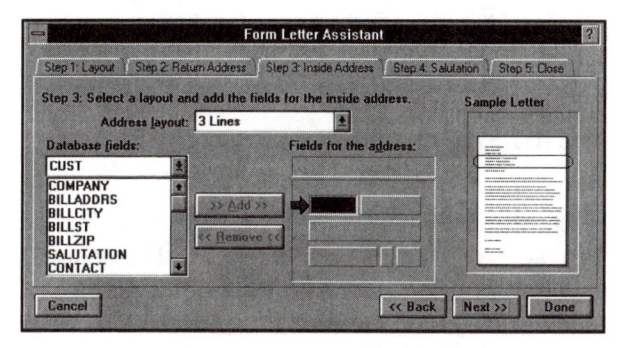

Figure 14.4 Select a layout and the fields to be included in it.

9. Select a layout from the Address layout drop-down list. In this case, Address refers to the recipient address that appears at the top of the letter.

10. Click on a field on the Database fields list. Then click on the gray rectangle that corresponds to the desired position for it in the inside address block and click on the >>Add button.

11. Repeat step 10 until the address block has been completely defined.

12. Click on the Next >> button to continue. The controls for Step 4 of the process appear (see Figure 14.5).

13. Click the button next to Dear and continue to step 14, or click on the None button to use no salutation and skip to step 15.

Lesson 14

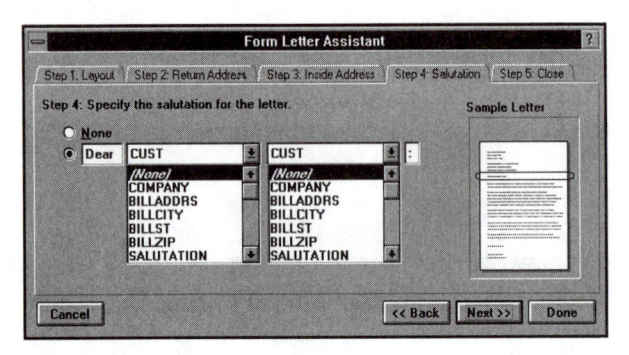

Figure 14.5 Define the salutation you want to use.

14. Select the field(s) to use for the salutation from the lists. For example, to use the title and last name (e.g. Mr. Jones), select TITLE from the first list and LASTNAME from the second list.

> **Using Only One Name?** To use a single name for the salutation (for example, Dear Donna), select the appropriate field from the first list and [None] from the second list.

15. Click on the Next >> button to continue. The controls for Step 5 of the process appear.

16. Type a closing for your form letter.

17. Click on the Done button to create your form letter.

Your form letter will now appear on the screen as another view. Approach has created a Form Letter view tab so you can see it whenever you want to.

Using a Form Letter

If you have been following along with the steps in this lesson, you now have an empty form letter, as shown in Figure 14.6.

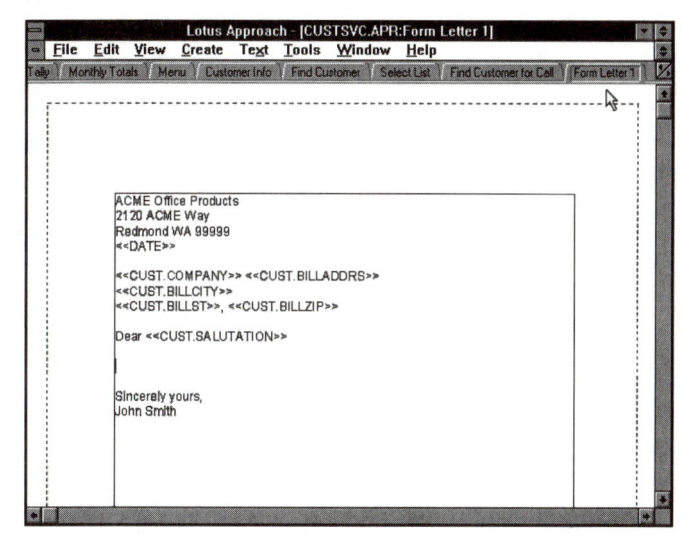

Figure 14.6 The generic form letter.

To use your new form letter, you need to complete the body of text in your letter and apply address records to the letter in mail-merge fashion. Here's how you use your empty form letter:

1. If your form letter is not the active view, click on its view tab to bring it into view.

2. Double-click on the document to select it. Click in the area of the form letter just below the Salutation and type in the body text of your message. Figure 14.7 shows you the same form letter with sample text.

3. Select Preview from the File menu to see your form letter with your database information filled in.

Lesson 14

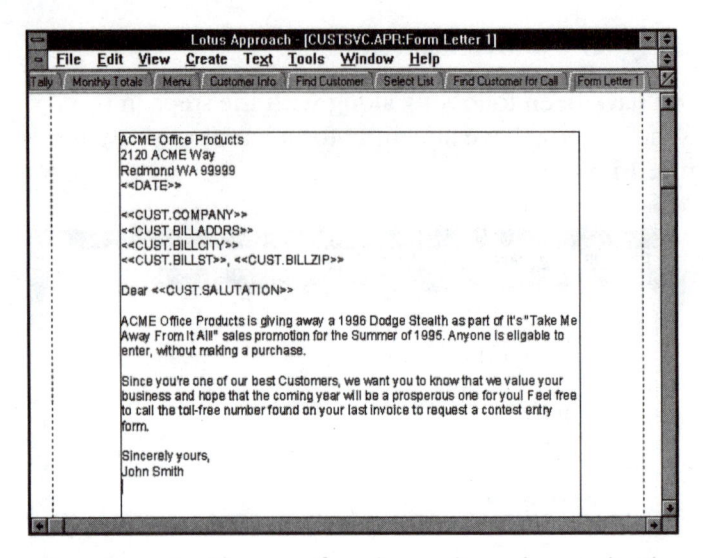

```
                    Lotus Approach - [CUSTSVC.APR:Form Letter 1]
    File  Edit  View  Create  Text  Tools  Window  Help
  Tally | Monthly Totals | Menu | Customer Info | Find Customer | Select List | Find Customer for Call | Form Letter 1

          ACME Office Products
          2120 ACME Way
          Redmond WA 99999
          <<DATE>>

          <<CUST.COMPANY>>
          <<CUST.BILLADDRS>>
          <<CUST.BILLCITY>>
          <<CUST.BILLST>>, <<CUST.BILLZIP>>

          Dear <<CUST.SALUTATION>>

          ACME Office Products is giving away a 1996 Dodge Stealth as part of it's "Take Me
          Away From It All" sales promotion for the Summer of 1995. Anyone is eligible to
          enter, without making a purchase.

          Since you're one of our best Customers, we want you to know that we value your
          business and hope that the coming year will be a prosperous one for you! Feel free
          to call the toll-free number found on your last invoice to request a contest entry
          form.

          Sincerely yours,
          John Smith
```

Figure 14.7 The same form letter, cleaned-up and with text added.

4. If you can't see the status bar, select Show Status Bar from the View menu.

5. Click on the right and left arrow buttons on the status bar to see the address information in your letter change to reflect the different records in your database.

6. Select Print from Approach's File menu. The Print dialog box appears.

7. Click on the Current form button to print only the displayed form letter or click on All to print a form letter for each recipient (as you specified when you made the form letter originally). Figure 14.8 shows the sample form letter.

Mailing Labels and Form Letters 87

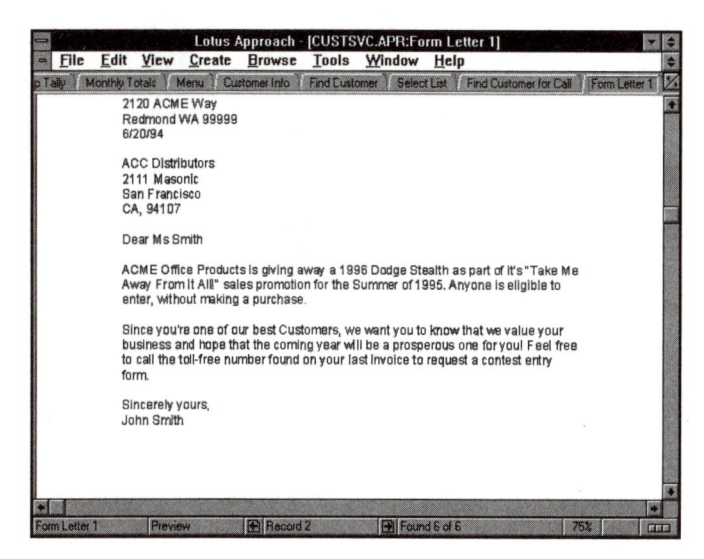

Figure 14.8 The finished form letter with a sample recipient.

In this lesson, you learned how to present the information located in your Approach files and databases. In the next lesson, you'll find out how to create a chart with your database information.

Lesson 15

Creating a Chart

In this lesson, you'll learn how to create a chart in Approach using the Chart Assistant.

Lotus Approach creates charts that rival many of the prominent charting software products available today. All you have to do is work through the charting process with Approach's Chart Assistant.

Creating a Chart

The process of creating a chart varies slightly based on the kind of chart you choose to make. In the following steps, we're going to create a 3-D bar chart.

Here's how you create a 3-D bar chart with Lotus Approach:

1. Open the Approach file or database file that contains the data you want to chart.

2. Select Chart from Approach's Create menu. The Chart Assistant dialog box opens (see Figure 15.1).

3. Type a title for your report in the View name & title text box.

4. Choose a style from the SmartMaster style drop-down list.

5. Choose a layout from the SmartMaster layout list (for example, choose 3-D Bar).

Creating a Chart 89

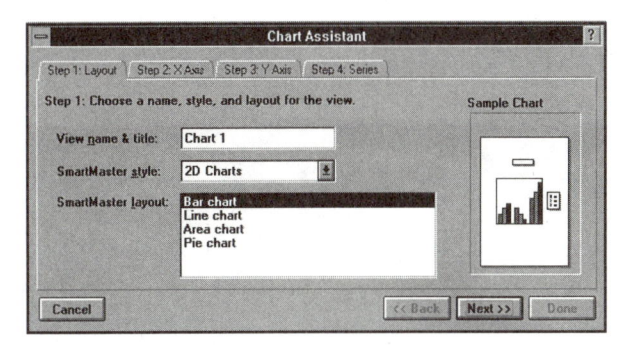

Figure 15.1 The Chart Assistant dialog box.

6. Click on the Next>> button to continue. The options for Step 2 appear (see Figure 15.2).

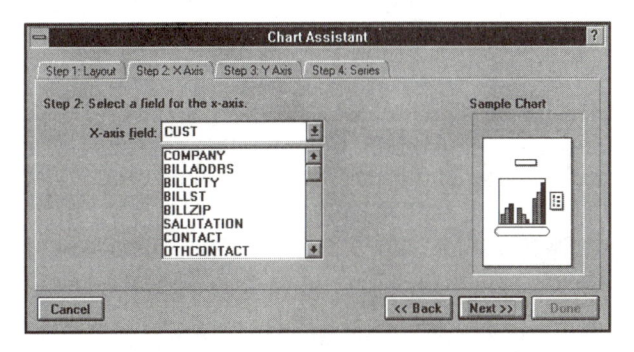

Figure 15.2 In Step 2, you select the X-axis field.

7. Choose the field that holds the data you want to present across the X axis (bottom) of your chart.

8. Click on the Next>> button to continue. The options for Step 3 appear, as shown in Figure 15.3.

9. Select the field that holds the information to be presented across the Y axis (the left side).

10. Click on the Next>> button to continue.

11. Click on the Done button. Lotus Approach displays your new chart on-screen.

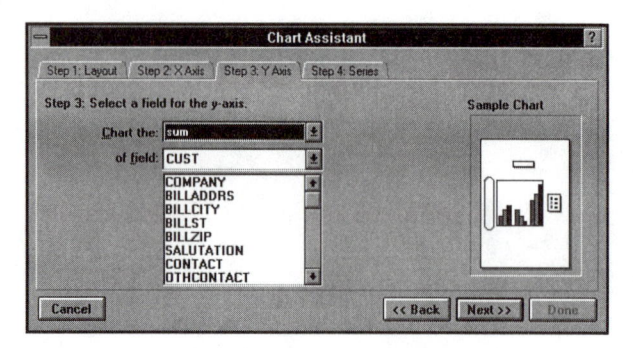

Figure 15.3 In Step 3, you select the Y-axis field.

If Approach needs to use fields from two or more databases, you will be asked to name just which databases contain the information to appear on the chart. You can change the database that's used if you make a mistake.

> **Go Easy!** You can easily present too much data on a single chart! Consider the primary point you want your chart to make. Keep charts as simple as you can while still presenting the necessary data.

Approach will create either 2-D or the more popular 3-D charts, depending on which you select in step 4. Users won't be able to tell the difference between charts created with Approach and those created with other sophisticated software products like Lotus 1-2-3 for Windows.

If your chart doesn't look quite like you want it to, you can modify it in Design mode, as you'll learn in Lesson 17. You can save and print your chart the same as you would any other part of your Approach file. (See Lesson 7 for help on saving; see Lesson 20 for help printing.)

In this lesson, you learned how to create a chart. In the next lesson, you'll learn to create a new form.

Lesson 16
Creating a Form

In this lesson, you'll learn to create additional forms.

Many views you've learned about so far in Approach, such as reports and charts, are used to present information to other people. In contrast, forms are mainly used to enter data into the database.

> **Form** An on-screen data entry form (much like a paper form you might fill out). Typically, the field names are displayed next to on-screen text boxes into which you can type field entries for one record at a time.
>
> *Plain English*

When you open or create a database, Approach automatically creates a form for you. It's called Form 1, and you use it to add and change records in the database. (See Lesson 10 to learn about adding records and Lesson 11 to learn about editing them.)

If you are not happy with Form 1, you can change it using Design mode (see Lesson 17). Or, if you want to create an alternative form to keep in addition to Form 1, you can create a new one. You can make as many forms as you like to enter information into a single database.

Creating a Form

To create a form, follow these steps:

1. Open the database or Approach file containing the data for which you want to create a new form.

2. Select Form from the Create menu. The Form Assistant dialog box appears (see Figure 16.1).

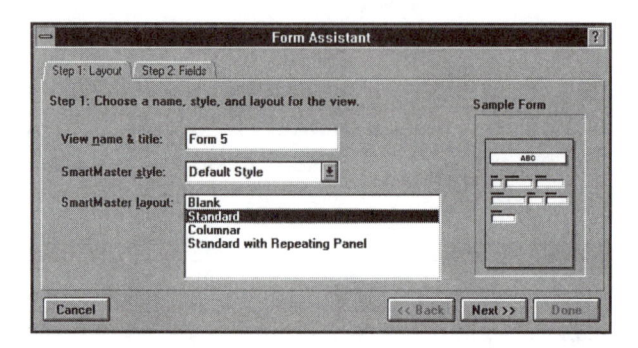

Figure 16.1 The Form Assistant dialog box.

3. Type a title for your form in the View name & title text box.

4. Choose a style from the SmartMaster style drop-down list.

5. Choose a layout from the SmartMaster layout list. For the purpose of this exercise, choose any type except Blank. (Blank does not enable you to select field names.)

> **Not So Fast!** SmartMaster Layouts are kind of like "prefab" page layouts for your forms. Experienced form wizards may want to start with a blank form and customize from scratch! As a beginner, you should select a basic form layout to make your life easier.

Creating a Form

The Case of the Disappearing Tab   Notice that, depending on the layout you select, different tabs appear at the top of the dialog box. This is because different layouts require different steps to complete them.

6. Click on the Next>> button to continue. The options for Step 2 appear (Figure 16.2).

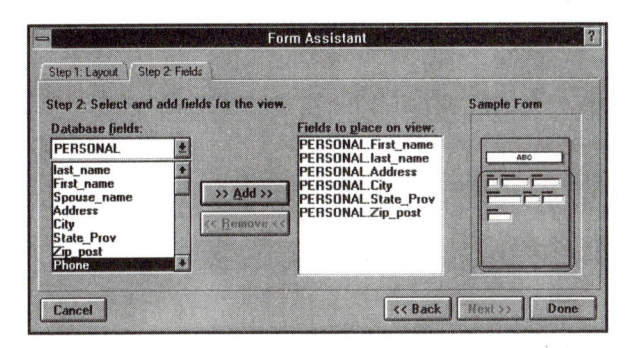

Figure 16.2   In Step 2, you select the fields to be included on the form.

7. Open the Database fields drop-down list and select the database from which you want to select fields. Unless you have joined databases (see Lesson 23) or are using an Approach sample file, there will be only one database on the list.

8. Click on the first field in the Database fields list to be included on the form. Then click the >>Add>> button to move it to the Fields to place on view list.

9. Continue adding fields to the list (as in step 8) until you have chosen all the fields you want to appear on the form.

Lesson 16

> **Use Those Keys!** To select multiple items that are listed together, click on the first item, press and hold the Shift key, and click on the last item. The first item, the last item, and all items in between are selected. To select multiple items that are not listed next to each other, hold down the Ctrl key and click on each item.

> **Why Is It Italicized?** Italicized field names indicate that the field's contents can be displayed on a form but cannot be edited.

10. If you chose Standard with Repeating Panel in step 5, a third step is needed; select Next>> and go to step 11. If not, select Done, and you're finished.

> **Repeating Panel** A repeating panel is simply a list made up of recurring fields. For example, you might have a customer that wants to order more than one item at one time. Each ordered item would be entered on the same order, but in consecutive sets of fields called repeating panels.

11. Select the fields to appear in the repeating panel, and then click the Done button.

When you're finished, the form appears on-screen, as shown in Figure 16.3. You can save and print this form the same as any other view; see Lessons 7 (for saving) and 21 (for printing).

Creating a Form 95

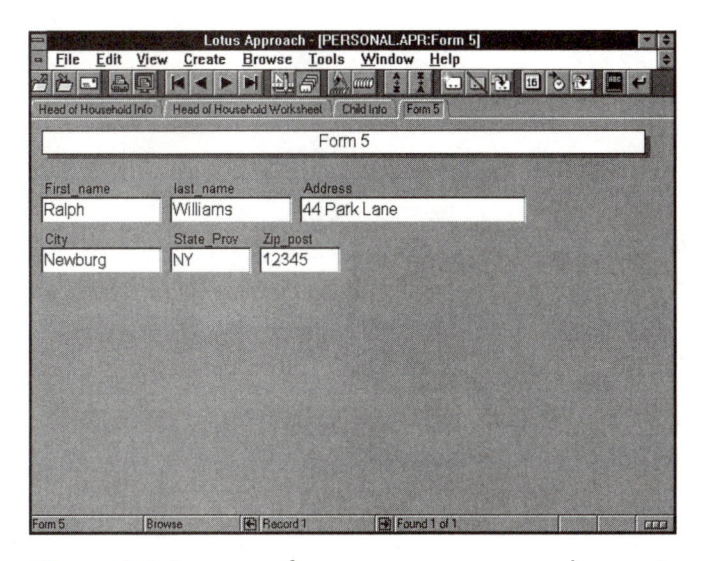

Figure 16.3 A new form appears on-screen when you've completed the steps.

Note that some fields cannot be accessed in the form. Those fields are denoted with lowercase labels. (These same field names were in italics on the Fields list when you were using Form Assistant.)

You can customize your form using Design mode; you'll learn about Design mode in the next lesson. You can further modify and add elements to forms by following the steps in Lessons 17 through 20.

In this lesson, you learned to create a form. In the next lesson, you'll learn how to use design mode to modify any view.

Lesson 17

Working with Design Mode

In this lesson, you'll learn how to modify any view using Design mode.

Once you create a view, you're not stuck with it. You can make many changes to a view. To do this, you enter Design mode. Design mode turns the view into a canvas of objects that you can move and alter.

You can edit all views in approximately the same way. In this lesson, we'll edit a form view, but you can use these same techniques in any view. In Lessons 19 and 20, you'll learn editing techniques specific to the form view.

Entering Design Mode

To enter Design mode, do one of the following:

- Click the Design SmartIcon.
- Open the View menu and select Design.
- Press Ctrl+D.

> Clicking the Design SmartIcon is the same as pressing Ctrl+D or selecting Design from the View menu.

Working with Design Mode

When your view is in Design mode, a floating palette of editing tools (the Tools palette) appears on-screen. In addition, a grid of tiny dots appears behind the objects in the view (see Figure 17.1).

> **Objects** Objects are the on-screen elements that you can move and size individually. In Design mode, each field, each graphic element, and each title is an object.

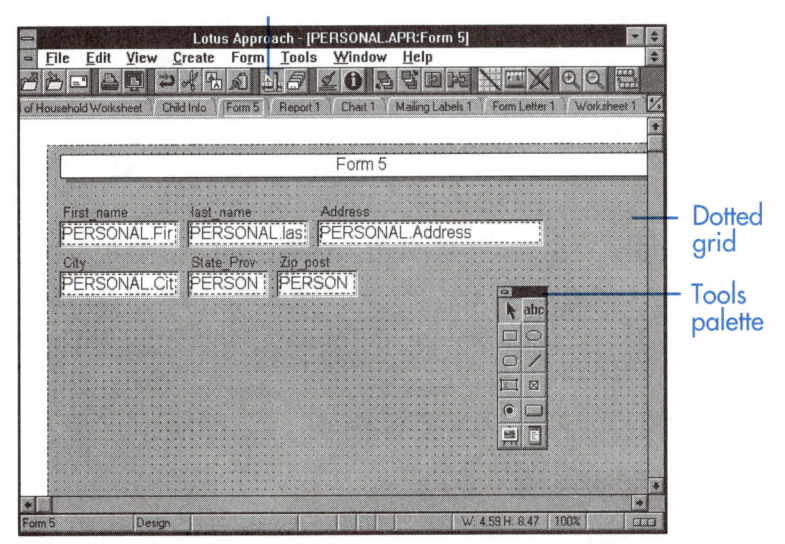

Figure 17.1 In Design mode, you can edit your view.

In Design mode, the SmartIcon palette changes somewhat, giving you a new set of SmartIcons with which to work. The SmartIcons that appear depend on the type of view you are editing. To find out what a SmartIcon does, point the mouse pointer at it, and a bubble will appear describing the SmartIcon.

Selecting an Object

To manipulate an object on-screen, you must first select it. Follow these steps to select an object:

1. If it is not already selected, click on the Arrow tool on the tool palette.

2. Click on the object to select it.

   To select more than one object at a time, hold down the Shift key while you click on multiple objects. When an object is selected, black or gray squares appear around it, as shown in Figure 17.2. These are called *selection handles* or just *handles*.

> **Plain English**
>
> **Handles** Squares that appear around an object, signifying that the object is selected and can be worked with.

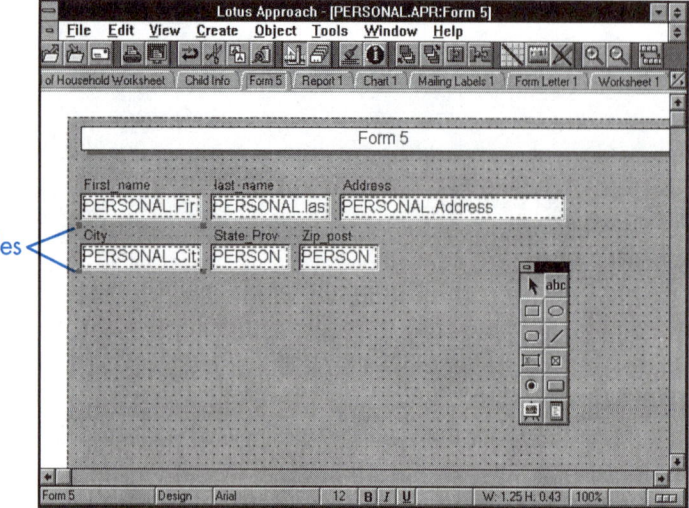

Figure 17.2 Selection handles appear around an object when you click on it.

Working with Design Mode

Moving an Object

To move an object around on-screen, follow these steps:

1. Select the object as described in the previous section.

2. Point to the selected object with the mouse pointer, and press and hold down the left mouse button. (Point somewhere in the middle of the object; do not point directly at a handle.)

3. Drag the object to the desired location. An outline shows where the object is going (see Figure 17.3).

4. Release the mouse button. The object is moved to the new location.

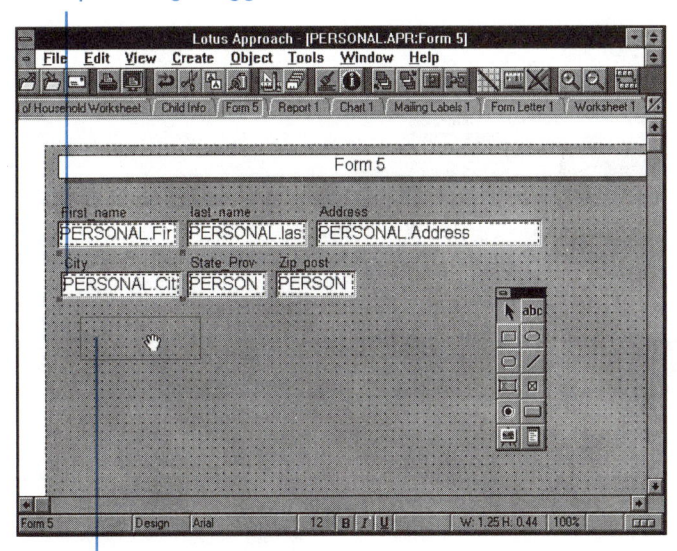

Figure 17.3 An outline rectangle shows where the object is being moved.

Lesson 17

Resizing an Object

To resize an object, drag one of its selection handles in the direction you want to go. To make an object smaller, drag a handle into its center; to make an object bigger, drag a handle away from it.

1. Select the object. Selection handles appear around it.

2. Move the mouse pointer over a handle; the mouse pointer changes to a double-headed arrow (see Figure 17.4).

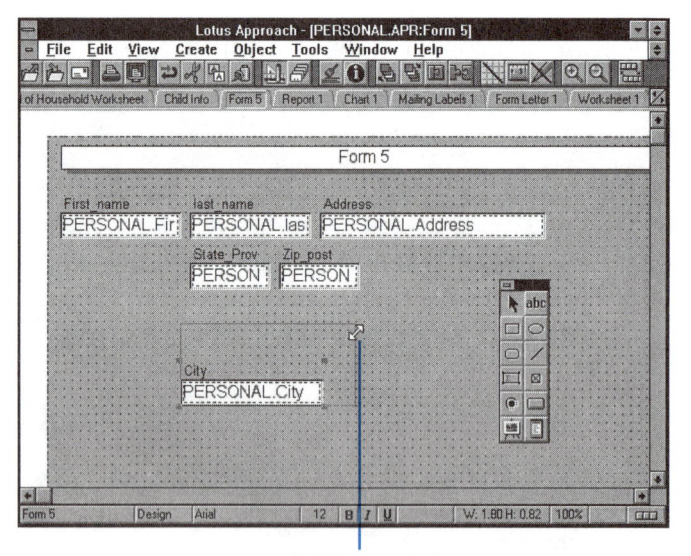

Double-headed arrow

Figure 17.4 A double-headed arrow indicates that you can drag to change the size of an object.

3. Click and hold the left mouse button, and drag the handle to resize the object. A rectangle outline shows where the object is going.

4. Release the mouse button when the rectangle is positioned the way you want the object.

Editing Text

To edit text in Design mode, follow these steps:

1. Click on the text to be edited. An insertion point (a blinking vertical line) appears in the text.

2. To delete text, either press Backspace to delete text to the left of the insertion point, or press Delete to delete text to the right of it. You can move the insertion point around in the text with the arrow keys.

3. Type new text as necessary.

4. Click outside the text to finalize your edits.

Changing Object Attributes

You can change all kinds of attributes for an object. When you double-click on an object, an InfoBox appears with options for that particular kind of object.

> **InfoBox** A dialog box that contains many settings you can change for the selected object. An InfoBox typically has several tabs, which you can click on to see other options.
>
> *Plain English*

The following steps show how to change the attributes of text, but it works much the same for any object.

1. Double-click on the edge of the object. An InfoBox appears (see Figure 17.5).

Control-menu box

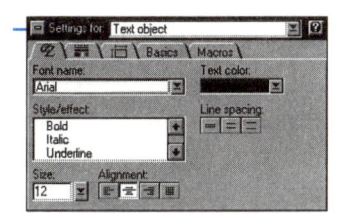

Figure 17.5 An InfoBox, in which you can specify various attributes for an object.

2. Change the options in the InfoBox. For instance, for a text object you can select a different font, style, color, spacing, size, and/or alignment.

> **What Are Those Other Tabs?** The InfoBox contains several tabs. Click on a different tab to see more attribute options.

3. When you are finished, double-click on the Control-menu box in the upper left corner of the InfoBox to close it.

Leaving Design Mode

There are two modes in Approach: Design mode and Browse mode. To leave Design mode, you simply switch back to Browse mode. You can do this in any of the following ways:

- Click the Browse SmartIcon.
- Press Ctrl+B.
- Select Browse from the View menu.

In this lesson, you learned to enter Design mode and make basic changes to your view. In the next lesson, you'll learn to add graphic objects to a view.

Lesson 18

Adding Graphics to a View

In this lesson, you'll learn how to add graphic images to an Approach view.

In the previous lesson, you saw how to manipulate the objects in a view to make them more visually appealing. You can also add graphics to a view, or draw your own graphics with Approach's built-in drawing tools. These graphic objects are not intended to be part of your database information—they're strictly for aesthetics.

You can even display a picture kept in a database record. Lotus Approach stores these images in PicturePlus fields.

Drawing Your Own Graphic Objects

When you enter Design mode, a palette of tools appears. Depending on which tool you select, your mouse pointer accomplishes different tasks. Table 18.1 shows each tool and tells what it does.

Table 18.1 The Tools Palette in Design Mode.

Tool	Function
▶	Selects objects
▢	Draws a rectangle

Lesson 18

Tool	Function
▢	Draws a rounded rectangle
	Creates a field
⦿	Creates a radio button
	Creates a PicturePlus field
abc	Creates a text box
○	Draws a circle or oval
/	Draws a line
☒	Creates a check box
▢	Creates a macro button
	Shows the Add Field dialog box

For now, just pay attention to the drawing tools, which are the lines and shapes. You will learn about some of the other tools later. Here's how to draw your own graphic objects:

1. Open the Approach file with which you want to work.

2. Switch to the view that is to receive the graphic object.

Need a Quick Refresher? Opening Approach files was covered in Lesson 8; changing views was covered in Lesson 6.

Adding Graphics to a View — 105

3. Click on the Design SmartIcon or select Design from the View menu. The design tools appear on your screen (see Figure 18.1).

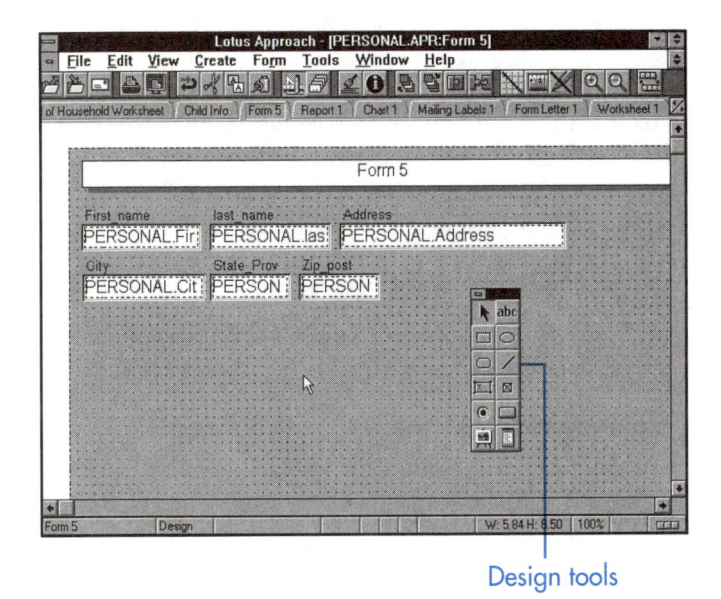

Figure 18.1 In Design mode, the design tools are ready for your use.

4. Click on a design tool to select it. For example, to draw a rectangle, click on the Rectangle tool.

5. On the view, click where you want to start the drawing.

6. Hold down the left mouse button and drag the mouse pointer to form the shape you want to draw.

7. When you are satisfied with the shape, release the left mouse button. The drawn object appears on-screen.

You can edit an object by double-clicking on it and using the InfoBox that appears, as you learned in Lesson 17.

You can change the thickness, color, and many other attributes using the InfoBox options.

Importing Graphics from Other Programs

If you have a different Windows-based graphics program you are comfortable with, you may prefer to use it instead of using Approach's drawing tools. Here's how to use a graphic created in another program in an Approach file:

1. Create the graphic in the graphics program of your choice (Paintbrush, for example).

2. Save the graphic, and exit the graphics program.

3. Start Approach if it's not already running.

4. Open the Approach file with which you want to work.

5. Switch to the view that is to receive the graphic object.

6. Click on the Design SmartIcon or select Design from the View menu to enter Design mode.

7. Choose Paste from File from the Edit menu. The Paste from File dialog box appears (Figure 18.2).

8. Open the List files of type drop-down list and select the graphic type you want to import.

9. Use the Drives and Directories lists to select the location of the file you want to import.

10. Select the file you want to import from the File name list.

11. Click on OK to import the file. The graphic appears on your Approach view, with selection handles around it.

Adding Graphics to a View

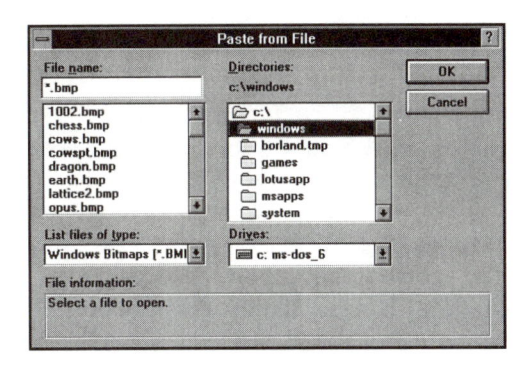

Figure 18.2 Choose a graphic to paste into Approach.

12. Reposition or resize the graphic as you learned in Lesson 17.

Cutting and Pasting Graphics

Just as with any text or graphic in a Windows-based program, you can cut and paste graphics in Approach. Here's how to use cut-and-paste to move a graphic from one Approach view to another:

1. Select the graphic.

2. Select Cut from the Edit menu. The graphic is cut to the Clipboard.

3. Display the view in which you want to paste the graphic.

4. Select Paste from the Edit menu. The graphic appears in the new view.

5. Resize or reposition the graphic as needed (see Lesson 17).

This procedure works equally well when pasting graphic images from Approach to another Windows-based program, or from another program into Approach.

Deleting Graphics

There are two ways to delete a graphic.

- Cut the graphic to the Clipboard, and then forget about it. When you cut something else later or shut down Windows, the image is destroyed.

or

- Select the image and press the Delete key.

Placing OLE Graphics in a View

Windows 3.1 (and higher) uses OLE or Object Linking and Embedding, a method of linking one file to another. To explain how linking works, let's first consider the process of importing a graphic. If you create your company logo in Paintbrush, *import* it into Approach, and then return to Paintbrush and make changes, the copy you imported into Approach becomes obsolete. (It does not contain the updated changes.) But if you *link* the company logo to the Approach file, every time you change the logo in Paintbrush, the copy in the Approach file changes too.

Creating an OLE Object

When you create a new OLE object, it is embedded in the Approach file. When you want to make changes to the object later, you can do so directly from Approach. Here's how you create and insert an embedded object into an Approach view:

1. Open the Approach file and view you want to use.

2. Switch to Design mode if you're not already there.

3. Select Object from the Create menu. The Insert Object dialog box appears, as in Figure 18.3.

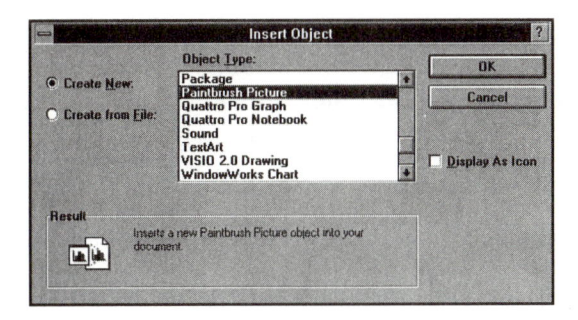

Figure 18.3 The Insert Object dialog box.

4. From the Object Type list, select the object type you want to create.

5. Click on the OK button. The application needed to create that object type opens.

6. Use that application to create your object.

7. Select Update from that application's File menu.

8. Select Exit & Return... from the File menu to switch back to Approach. The graphic object appears in Approach, with selection handles around it to indicate it is selected.

9. Reposition or resize the object as desired.

In the future, you can make changes to this object in Approach by double-clicking on it. The application will reopen so that you can make changes. Since it does not have a name of its own (it was a new drawing and you didn't save it by its own name), you cannot view or edit the graphic file except while in Approach.

Linking or Embedding an Existing Object

If you have already created a graphic object in another program, you may want to insert it into an Approach view instead of recreating it from scratch. You can embed it, as described in the previous steps, so that you can edit it later from within Approach. Or you can link it, so that changes you make to the graphic while not in Approach will be automatically reflected in the Approach file.

Follow these steps to link or embed an existing object:

1. Open the Approach file and view you want to use.

2. Switch to Design mode if you're not already there.

3. Select Object from the Create menu. The Insert Object dialog box appears, as in Figure 18.3.

4. Select the Create from File radio button. The Insert Object dialog box changes to look like Figure 18.4.

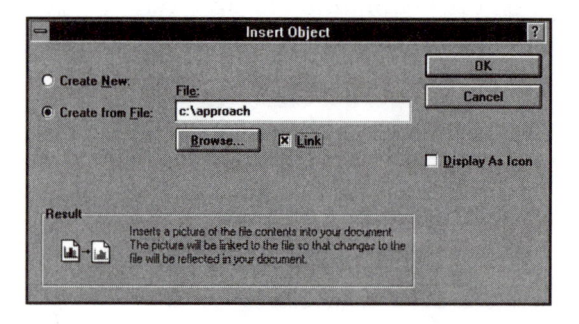

Figure 18.4 The Insert Object dialog box changes if you want to insert an existing file.

5. If you know the exact name and location of the file, type it in the File text box. (If you don't know the file's exact name and location, click the Browse button and use the dialog box that appears to search for the file.)

6. If you want to link the file, click the Link check box.

7. Select OK. The graphic appears in Approach.

8. Reposition or resize the object as desired.

Adding Graphics to a View 111

Creating Stacked Graphics

There may be times when you need to overlap multiple graphical images that have been pasted into a view. You may choose to present one graphic on top of another graphic for effect, or to simply fit two images into a small piece of real estate on your screen.

When you create or paste a new image onto a view, it always appears "on top." You can change that default placement. The concept is called *stacking*, and is shown in Figure 18.5. Here's how you establish the order in which stacked images appear:

White box stacked on top of black box

Figure 18.5 Several graphics can be stacked to create interesting effects.

1. Open the Approach file and the view that contain the graphic objects.

2. Switch to Design mode by selecting Design from the View menu or by clicking the Design SmartIcon.

3. Select the object for which you want to change the stacking order.

4. Select Arrange from the Object menu.

5. Select from one of these menu items to arrange the selected graphic:

   - **Bring to Front**   Moves an object to the foreground.

   - **Send to Back**   Moves an object to the background.

- **Bring Forward** Moves an object one level toward the foreground.
- **Send Backward** Moves an object one level toward the background.

You can repeat this set of steps on any graphic object you select, even those that are under five or more stacked graphic images.

In this lesson, you learned how to insert graphic objects into Approach views. In the next lesson, you'll learn how to further customize your data entry forms.

Lesson 19

Making Your Forms Easier to Use

In this lesson, you'll learn how to customize the forms that you use to enter data into your database so that they are easier to use.

The default form that Approach creates is straightforward, but is not always easy to use. It takes effort to customize your form to make it a useful and attractive data entry screen. With a little practice, you can create sophisticated forms like the samples included with Approach. In this lesson, you'll see some of the ways you can make your forms more useful and appealing.

Changing the Tab Order of the Fields

Most Windows applications (including Approach) let you use the Tab key to toggle between fields or other screen options such as text boxes and radio buttons. In Approach, you can change the order in which you Tab through fields in a form.

Here's how you customize the order in which the Tab key toggles you between form fields:

1. Open an Approach file and select the form for which you want to change the Tab order.

2. Select Show Data Entry Order from the View menu. Gray text boxes appear over every field (except the ones you can't access, if there are any). Figure 19.1 shows an Approach file with the gray text boxes.

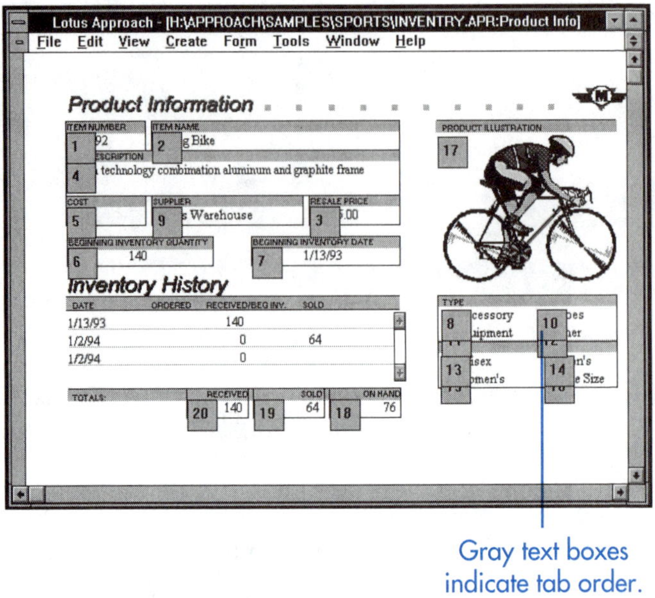
Lotus Approach - [H:\APPROACH\SAMPLES\SPORTS\INVENTRY.APR:Product Info]
File Edit View Create Form Tools Window Help
Product Information
Inventory History
Gray text boxes indicate tab order.

Figure 19.1 Tab order text boxes.

3. Place the insertion point into any gray text box and change the number displayed there.

4. Click on any other gray text box and change its number, until all numbers have been changed to the order you desire.

> **Number Them All!** You can't leave a field out of the sequence; if you do not specify a number in one of the gray text boxes, that field will be assigned the number "1" by default.

5. Select Browse from the View menu and try using the Tab key to toggle between fields in the order you specified.

Using an InfoBox to Format Fields

Lotus Approach packs several field formatting options into a single dialog box called *InfoBox*. (You saw some InfoBoxes in Lessons 17 and 18.) With an InfoBox, you can easily change the font, size, or color of text in a field.

You open an InfoBox by double-clicking on any screen object while in Design mode. The InfoBox that appears is tailored to the type of screen object you selected. The following steps show how to use an InfoBox to format a field:

1. Open an Approach file and switch to the form you want to change.

2. Select Design from the View menu to switch to Design mode.

3. Double-click on the field you want to change. The InfoBox opens. Figure 19.2 shows the InfoBox for the Item Description field in our example form.

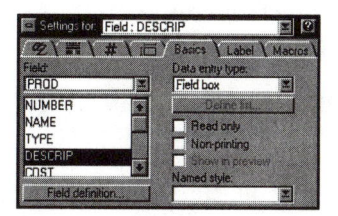

Figure 19.2 An InfoBox for a field.

Doing It All! You're not limited to working with just fields. You can use an InfoBox to change just about every screen object on a Form.

4. Change any of the settings in the InfoBox. Click on one of the other tabs to see more settings.

5. Double-click the Control-menu box in the upper left corner of the InfoBox when you're finished making changes.

On the Basics tab of the InfoBox (the one that is displayed first), you can select which field you're formatting. By default it's the one you double-clicked on, but you can pick a different field to format several without closing the InfoBox.

The InfoBox contains too many options to list them all here; experiment with each tab to see what it has to offer.

Creating Radio Buttons

You can create radio buttons to be used during the data entry process. Adding radio buttons is a great way to limit the number of ways people can make errors while adding information to a database. For example, if a data entry person must select from a list of predefined types, you can display a radio button for each type to limit the amount of memorization needed.

Here's how you create radio buttons to use for filling in your database information:

1. Open the Approach file and display the form for which you want to add radio buttons.

2. Select Design from the View menu to enter Design mode.

3. Double-click on the field that you want to change to a radio button. An InfoBox opens.

4. Select the field you want to change, and then click on the down-arrow next to the Data entry type text box to see a list of screen objects. Select Radio buttons from that list. The Define Radio Buttons dialog box appears, as shown in Figure 19.3.

Making Your Forms Easier to Use   **117**

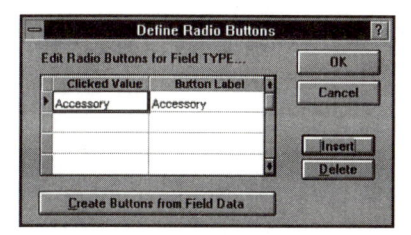

Figure 19.3 The Define Radio Buttons dialog box.

5. Under Clicked Value, specify the entry to be inserted into your database field when the radio button is selected.

6. Under Button Label, type the text you want displayed next to the radio button.

7. Click on the OK button. The radio buttons appear on your form.

> **From Field Data?** If you want to have Approach create button labels from actual information kept in the fields, click on the Create Buttons from Field Data button.

Aligning Fields on a Form

As you are repositioning the fields on your form (Lesson 17), you may find it difficult to get fields perfectly aligned with one another. Misaligned fields look messy, and distract the user. Figure 19.4 shows an example of a newly created form with misaligned fields.

Approach can help you align the fields precisely. Simply follow these steps:

1. Open the Approach file and select the view that you want to work with.

Lesson 19

2. Enter Design mode by clicking the Design SmartIcon or by selecting Design from the Create menu.

3. Select the fields to be aligned. Selection handles should appear around each selected field.

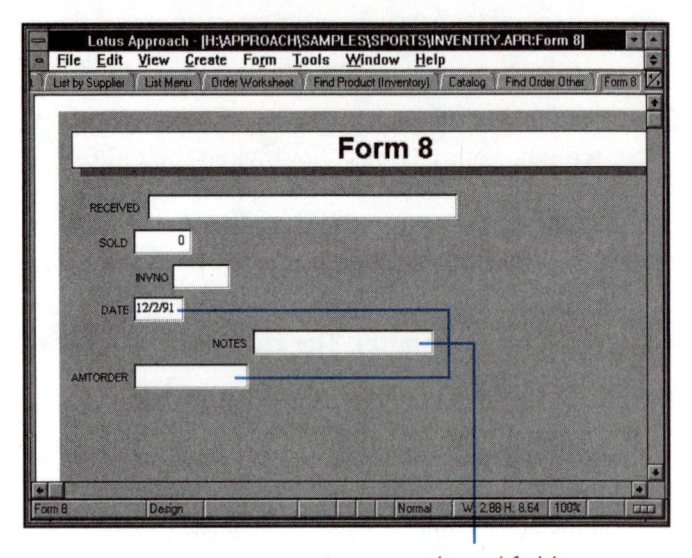

Misaligned fields

Figure 19.4 Misaligned fields on a form.

Selecting Fields There are two ways to select multiple fields. The slow way is to click on a field (so that selection handles appear around it), and then hold down the Shift key while you click on other fields. The fast way is to "draw" a box with the mouse pointer around the fields. Click and hold in one corner of the area that contains the fields, and drag the mouse pointer to the opposite corner. When you release the mouse button, selection handles appear around each selected field.

Making Your Forms Easier to Use 119

4. Select Align from the Object menu. The Align dialog box opens (Figure 19.5).

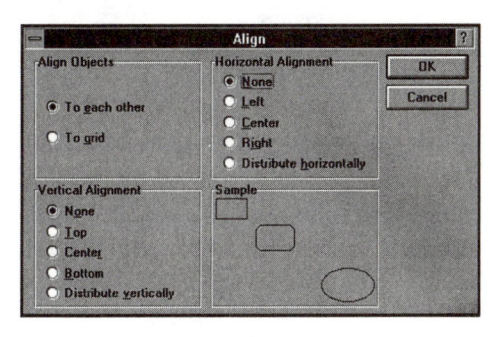

Figure 19.5 The Align dialog box.

5. Choose between aligning the objects with each other or aligning them to a grid.

6. Specify Horizontal and Vertical alignment options. Keep an eye on the geometric objects in the Sample group box to see how your selections will affect your fields.

7. Click on the OK button when you're ready to apply your preferences to the selected fields.

Your fields will now be distributed in a sensible fashion according to the options you selected in the Align dialog box.

In this lesson, you learned to make your form more attractive and easy to use by changing the tab order, using the InfoBox, adding radio buttons, and aligning the fields. In the next lesson, you'll learn to print.

Lesson 20

Printing Your Data

In this lesson, you'll learn how to print the data and views you create in Approach.

The whole point of creating reports, labels, form letters, and so on is to print and use them in hard copy form. Printing in Approach is straightforward and works much like printing in any other Windows-based program.

Previewing before Printing

Approach enables you to see how your printed page will look before you print it. If you're satisfied with the page's appearance, you go on to print the page. If you want to make more changes, it's "back to the drawing board" for you!

Here's how you preview a page before you print it:

1. Open the Approach file and view that you want to print.

2. Select Preview from the File menu. This will cause Approach to zoom out so you can see most of the page on-screen (as it will be printed).

3. Place the pointer over the page. Click on the left mouse button to zoom in; click on the right mouse button to zoom out. Figure 20.1 shows you a single page from a sample catalog, as you could expect it to print.

Printing Your Data   **121**

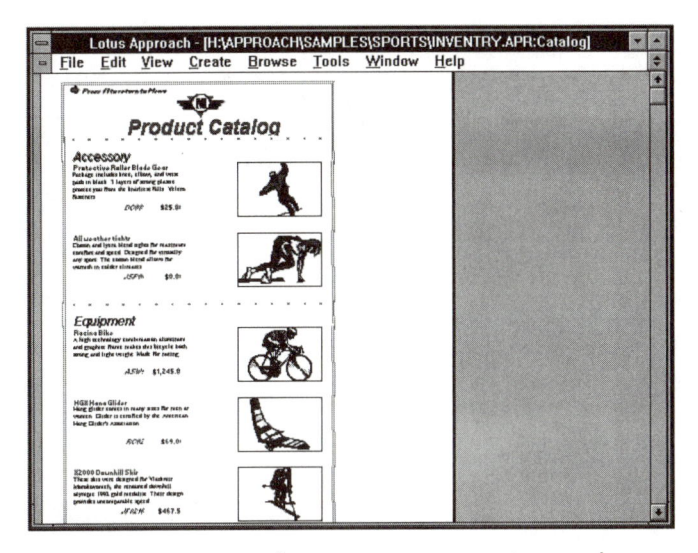

Figure 20.1   A catalog page seen in preview mode.

Save Time   You can see every other view while you're in preview mode. Just select any other view (by clicking on another view tab) to see it as it will print.

4. Select Browse from the View menu to end using preview.

Printing a View

The procedure for printing any view is the same—learn one printing method and you've learned them all. Here's how you print a view:

1. Open an Approach file and select the view you want to see and print. For this example, I'm using the sample view shown in Figure 20.2.

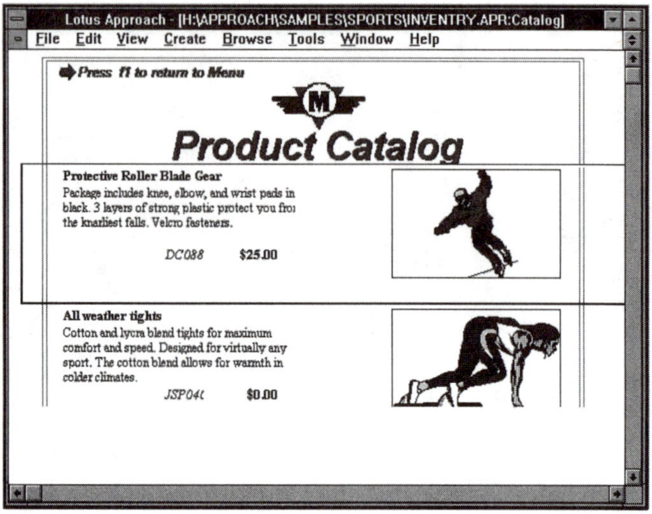
Lotus Approach - [H:\APPROACH\SAMPLES\SPORTS\INVENTRY.APR:Catalog]
File Edit View Create Browse Tools Window Help
Press f1 to return to Menu
Product Catalog
Protective Roller Blade Gear
Package includes knee, elbow, and wrist pads in black. 3 layers of strong plastic protect you fro
the knarliest falls. Velcro fasteners.
DC088
$25.00
All weather tights
Cotton and lycra blend tights for maximum comfort and speed. Designed for virtually any sport. The cotton blend allows for warmth in colder climates.
$0.00

Figure 20.2 A single page of a sample catalog.

2. Select Print from the File menu. The Print dialog box opens, as shown in Figure 20.3.

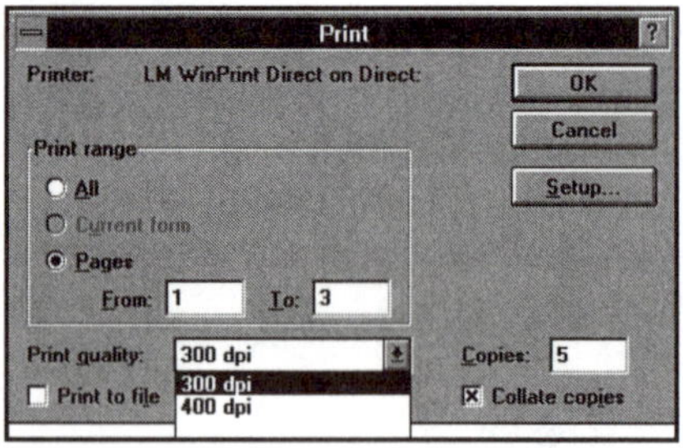
Print
Printer: LM WinPrint Direct on Direct
OK
Cancel
Setup...
Print range
All
Current form
Pages
From: 1
To: 3
Print quality: 300 dpi
300 dpi
400 dpi
Print to file
Copies: 5
Collate copies

Figure 20.3 The Print dialog box.

3. Under Print range, select the range of pages to print. You can print all pages, a range of pages, or various selected pages.

4. If your printer supports this option, you can choose between different levels of Print quality. Figure 20.3 shows the quality levels available for the laser printer I am using.

Printing Your Data   **123**

> **Highest Isn't Always Best**   If the view you're about to print contains bitmaps that must be printed as levels of gray, consider printing at less than the maximum print quality. Some laser printers will produce better-looking print quality at 300 dpi (dots-per-inch) than they will at 400 dpi or higher—especially when printing graphics.

5. Click on the Print to File check box if you want to create a file instead of printing on paper. If you choose this option, you'll be prompted for a file name to use for your "printed" output.

6. If you are printing multiple copies of multiple pages, click on the Collate copies check box to have your printer produce one multiple-page document at a time.

7. Select the number of copies you want to print. The default is 1.

8. Click on the OK button to print your materials.

> **Poor Graphics Printout?**   If you're not getting good quality printouts of your graphics, check the setup options. (Click the Setup button in the Print dialog box.) Make sure the Image Quality is set for High or Fine or some variation (depending on your printer).

Changing the Print Setup

Many people have more than one printer. For example, you might have a dot-matrix printer for multiple-part forms, a laser printer for letters and memos, and a color printer for transparencies and reports. It's easy to switch among your printers in Approach. You can also easily change the options for any printer, including the paper orientation, paper size, darkness, graphics quality, and font cartridges.

Install First! Before you can use a printer with Windows, you must install a driver for it. To install a printer driver, in the Control Panel (located in the Main program group) in Windows, select Printers and use the dialog box that appears to add a printer. For detailed instructions on adding a printer, see your Windows documentation.

Here's how you change the current printer or its printing options:

1. Open an Approach file.

2. Select Print Setup from the File menu. The Print Setup dialog box opens (see Figure 20.4). The printers connected to your PC will probably be different from mine (Figure 20.4).

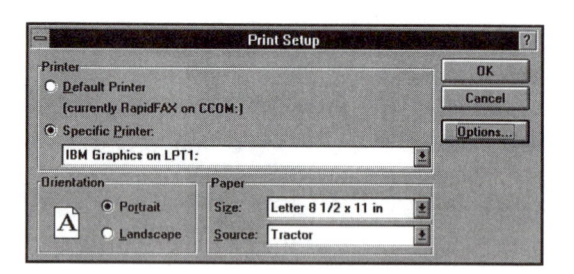

Figure 20.4 The Print Setup dialog box.

3. If you want to use the default printer, click on the Default Printer radio button.

4. If you want to use a printer other than the default printer, click on the Specific Printer radio button. Then click on the down arrow next to the specific

Printing Your Data 125

printer listed to see a list of other installed printers. Click on one of the installed printers to select it.

5. Select the paper orientation—either Portrait or Landscape—and select the paper size and source.

6. Click on the Options button to see the specific options available for your printer. Change any options you want, and then click OK to return to the Print Setup dialog box.

7. Click on the OK button.

Some Printer Setup dialog boxes will expand to offer more features and functions than others. The number of available options and features depends entirely on which printer is currently selected.

In this lesson, you learned all about printing with Approach. In the next lesson, you'll find out how you can customize the way data is entered into your databases.

Lesson 21

Working with Numbers

In this lesson, you'll learn how to work with the numbers stored in your databases.

Many of us collect information in the form of dollar amounts, quantities of items, numbers of occurrences, and so on. Approach enables you to work with numbers in two ways. You can create a *calculated field* to hold the results of your additions, subtractions, and so on, or you can simply *summarize* information on a report, worksheet, or crosstab.

Summarizing

If you're just repeating numbers so people can see totals, summarizing is what you need to do. Approach lets you summarize quantities in reports, worksheets, and crosstabs.

Approach displays summarized information in a *panel* directly adjacent to the body of text. Since most people want summarized information to appear on reports they create, this next set of steps will detail how to add a summary panel to a report:

1. Open the Approach file that contains the report to which you want to add the summary panel.

2. Switch to the report view that you want to summarize. (Click on its view tab.)

3. Select Design from the View menu or click on the Design SmartIcon to switch to Design mode.

Working with Numbers

4. Open the Create menu and choose Summary. The Summary dialog box opens (see Figure 21.1).

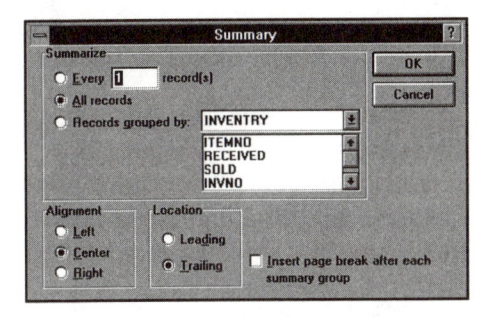

Figure 21.1 The Summary dialog box.

5. Choose one of the following Summarize options:

Every ___ Records (fill in the number) adds a summary every so many records.

All records adds a summary for each record individually.

Records grouped by (select a field name) adds summaries with the records grouped by the two previous options.

6. Click on one of the Alignment option buttons (Left, Center, or Right) to specify where you want the summary panel located on the report.

7. If you want the summary panel to appear before each group of summarized records, click on the Leading option button. If you want your summary panel displayed after the records you want to summarize, click on the Trailing option button.

128   Lesson 21

8. If you want each group of summarized records displayed (with the summary panel) on a page of its own, click on the Insert page break after each summary group check box.

9. Click on the OK button to create the summary panel.

Your summary panel appears on your report. Figure 21.2 shows an example of trailing summary panels placed every five records.

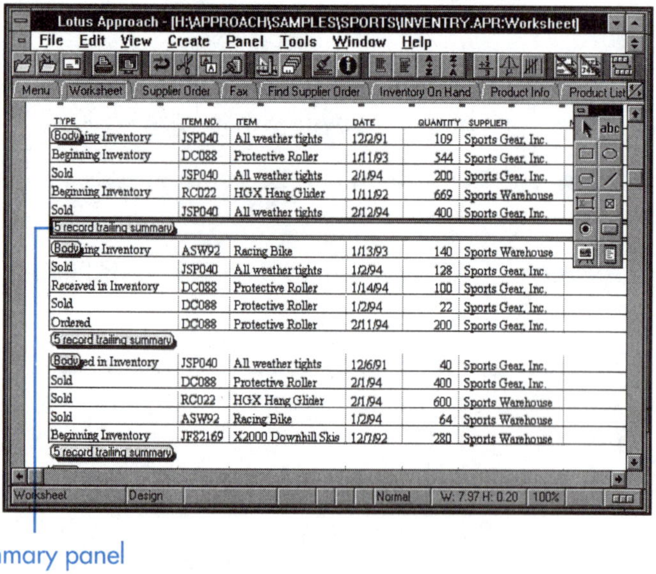

Summary panel

Figure 21.2   Five-record summary panels.

Using Calculated Fields

If you have to apply real math to numbers, like calculating sales tax or other percentages, you'll need to create a *calculated field* for your database records, and then display it in your views. Figure 21.3 shows you examples of calculated fields on a typical order form.

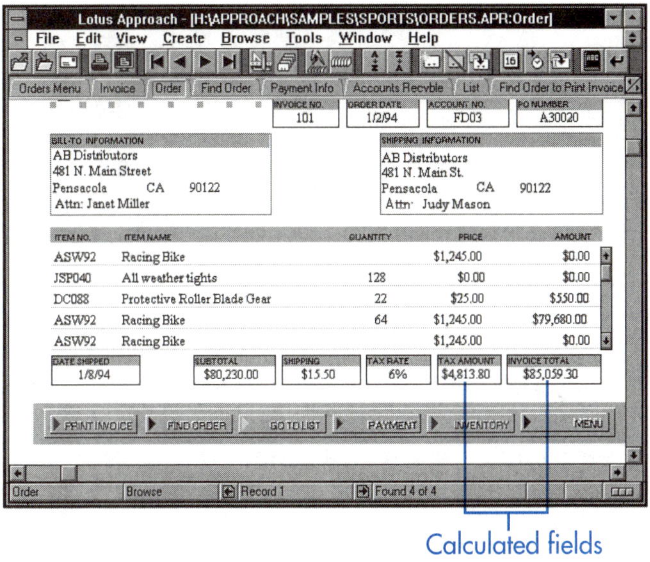

Figure 21.3 Calculated fields on a form.

Creating a Calculated Field

To create a calculated field in a report or other view, you must first create a calculated field in your database. For example, you could add up a set of numbers found in the same field in every record in your database, and then repeat that number on a form or report.

Here's how you add a calculated field to your database:

1. Open the Approach file or database to which you want to add a calculated field.

2. Switch to the view that will display your new calculated field.

3. Open the Create menu and select Field Definition. The Field Definition dialog box appears (Figure 21.4).

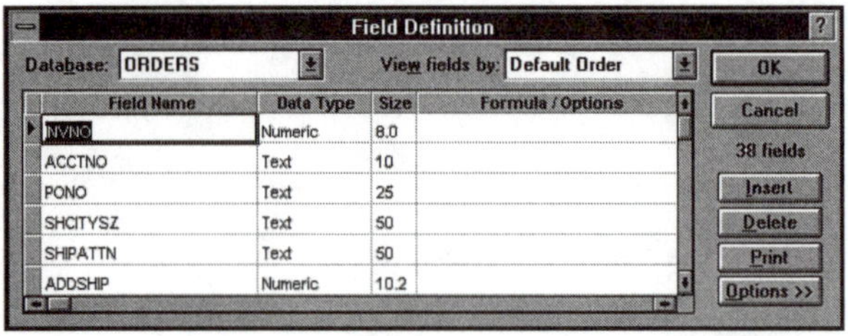
Field Definition
Database: ORDERS
View fields by: Default Order
OK
Cancel
38 fields
Insert
Delete
Print
Options >>
Field Name
Data Type
Size
Formula / Options
INVNO Numeric 8.0
ACCTNO Text 10
PONO Text 25
SHCITYSZ Text 50
SHIPATTN Text 50
ADDSHIP Numeric 10.2

Figure 21.4 The Field Definition dialog box.

Name That Host! If you are using multiple databases in your calculation, you'll need to select which databases will be the host of your new calculated field.

4. Select the database that is to receive the new calculated field. (In most cases, it will be the same as the database you opened in step 1.)
5. Review the list of fields and decide where (in the field order) you want to place the calculated field you're about to add.
6. Click on the field name that should follow the calculated field you're about to add, and then click on the Insert button to add the new field. To make your new calculated field the last field on the list, click on the empty field at the end of the list.
7. Click on the empty Field Name text box and enter the name of your new field. Next, click on the Data Type field and choose Calculated from the list of Data Types. The Field Definition dialog box expands so that you can further define your new calculated field (see Figure 21.5).

Working with Numbers   **131**

8. Select the first field that you want to use in your calculations, and then choose an operator or function. Repeat the process for each field you want to use. Figure 21.5 shows a simple formula used in an order form to determine the total amount due, after tax and shipping.

Field list

[Field Definition dialog box]

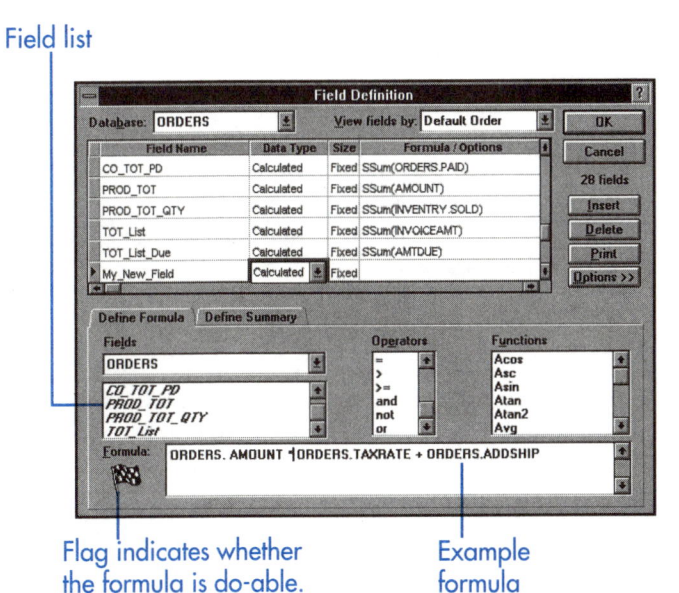

Flag indicates whether the formula is do-able.   Example formula

Figure 21.5 The Field Definition dialog box expands to show calculated field options.

Watch for the Flag! The flag displayed to the left of the Formula text box tells you if your formula is "do-able." If your formula will work, the checkered flag is clearly displayed. If your formula won't work, the flag will be grayed and will have a red X superimposed on it!

9. Click on the OK button.

10. When the Add Field dialog box appears, drag-and-drop your new calculated field name onto its new home on the selected view.

You can use any combination of field names, operators, and functions to create your formula.

> **Formula Shortcuts** Look at the sample databases included on your Approach disks to see how other formulas similar to your own were devised to "crunch numbers." You can cut and paste those formulas into the Formula text box and make your job a little easier.

In this lesson, you learned how to work with numbers in your databases. In the next lesson, you'll learn how to validate data input to make that data more accurate.

Lesson 22

Validating Data Input

In this lesson, you'll learn how to validate your data input to prevent errors.

Minimizing Data Entry Errors with Validated Fields

People inevitably make mistakes when typing data into a database. For example, decimal places are often left out or misplaced within a number. Or too many or too few zeros are used in a number. These mistakes can make your calculated results inaccurate, can cause sorting problems, and more.

Approach enables you to "validate" the information that's added to your databases. Approach can limit the type of data entered into a field to make sure it's the *kind* of data that belongs there (for example, making sure you enter a date in the field for today's date). Approach can also help you make sure that the right *form* of the right data is committed to your database, which reduces typos and transcription errors that all humans make.

Types of Validation

There are several ways you can restrict the contents of a field to validate it. Here are your choices:

Unique Make each entry unique. For example, you might make your customer order number field unique to ensure that no two orders had the same number.

From/To Make each entry fall into a "to/from" range. For example, you might set a limit of 00000 to 99999 for ZIP codes; any number that is not five digits would not qualify.

Filled in Requires some kind of data in this field for each record. (Other database programs refer to this as a "mandatory field.")

One of Tell Approach that data entered must appear on the One of: list. For example, if there were several valid entries for a field, you could list them all here, and Approach would exclude all other entries.

Formula is true If the formula you enter is true, the value is accepted; if not, it's rejected. For instance, you could have a formula such as >0 which would exclude all negative numbers.

In field Make sure that the entry matches an existing entry. This option is useful if you always ship to the same address to which you invoice. You can use the contents of another field in any database.

> **Click Once!** One of the best ways to validate data during input is to create radio buttons and check boxes whenever it works for your form. You learned to do this in Lesson 19.

Validating Data Input 135

Setting Up Field Validation

In this set of steps, we'll use Approach's validation feature to make sure ZIP codes are entered correctly.

1. Open the Approach or database file that contains the data you want to validate. For this example, pick one that contains ZIP codes.

2. Switch to Design mode (choose Design from the View menu or click on the Design SmartIcon).

3. Select Field Definition from the Create menu. The Field Definition dialog box opens.

4. Click on the Options>> button to expand the size of the dialog box.

5. Click on the Validation tab. Figure 22.1 shows you an expanded Field Definition dialog box with the Validation tab options showing.

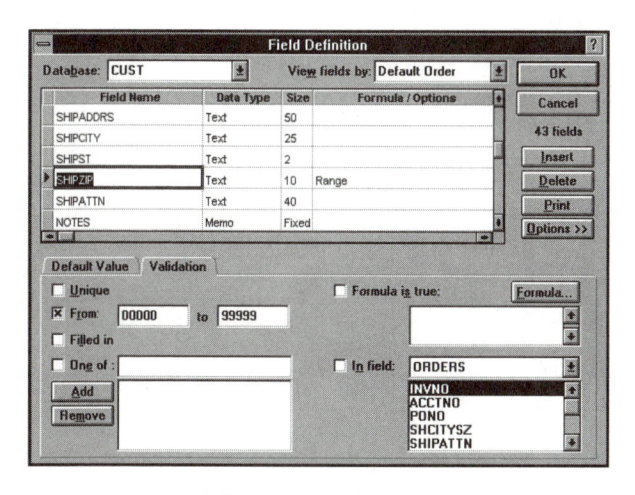

Figure 22.1 Validating a field.

6. Click the From check box, and enter 00000 and 99999 in the text boxes.

7. Click on the OK button to finish.

Your data input process will be smoother and safer now that you've forced more accurate data to be input to your databases.

In this lesson, you learned how to validate data input. In the next lesson, you'll learn how to present your information more effectively.

Lesson 23

Joining Files

In this lesson, you'll learn how to join Approach database files.

Different Types of Database Programs

There are two main kinds of database software. One kind allows you to work with a single database file. The other kind allows you to work with several files at one time, as though they were all a single file. Programs that fall into the former category are called *flat-file* databases. Products that handle several databases as though they were one are called *relational* databases.

Flat-file database programs are adept at managing lots of info as though they were actually working with a two dimensional spreadsheet with rows and columns. Relational database programs enable you to connect or relate several databases so that you can work with them as one. You don't have to make changes to every database you have if the same info occurs in several. Approach relates your databases to prevent you from having redundant data entry chores. For the nontechnical among us, Lotus Approach refers to the relating of databases as "joining."

Joining Approach Files

If you have two databases that contain the same basic type of information, you may want to join them so that changes you make in one database are reflected in the second. The process is simple. You open two databases and tell Approach which field(s) the two databases have in common. Here's how you join two databases:

1. Open one of the two Approach (or database) files that you want to join.

2. Select Join from the Create menu. The Join dialog box opens, as shown in Figure 23.1.

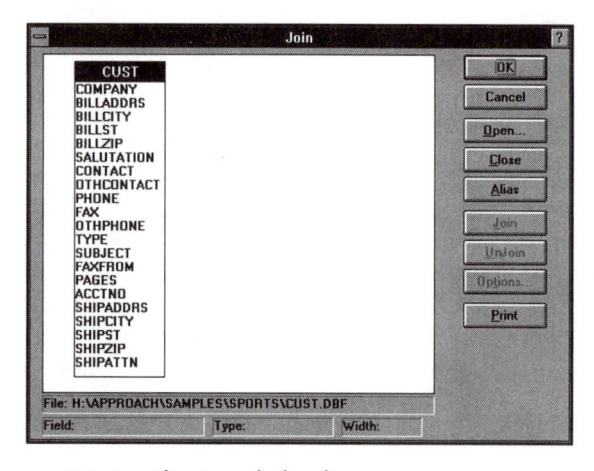

Figure 23.1 The Join dialog box.

3. Click on the Open button and select a second database file from the Open dialog box. Click OK to open the second database file you want to join. Figure 23.2 shows the Join dialog box with a second customer-related database opened.

4. If you see two fields that hold the same information, like a customer's company name, for example, drag from one field to the matching field in the second database. A line appears, indicating that you've established a link between these two fields in the databases.

5. Join other fields in the database if you want, and then click on the OK button to save your work.

Joining Files

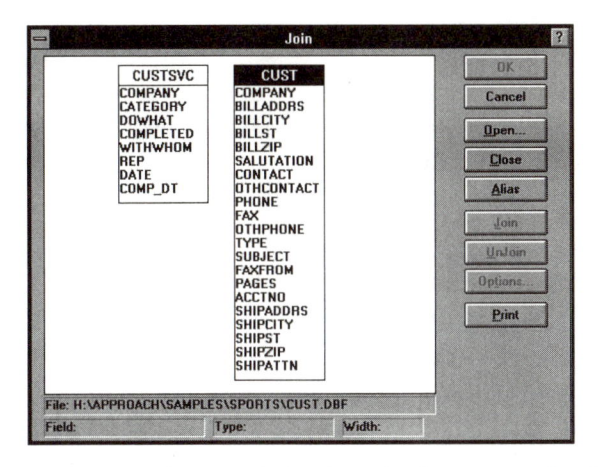

```
                      Join
    ┌─CUSTSVC──┐  ┌──CUST────┐        OK
    │COMPANY   │  │COMPANY   │      Cancel
    │CATEGORY  │  │BILLADDRS │
    │DOWHAT    │  │BILLCITY  │      Open...
    │COMPLETED │  │BILLST    │
    │WITHWHOM  │  │BILLZIP   │      Close
    │REP       │  │SALUTATION│
    │DATE      │  │CONTACT   │      Alias
    │COMP_DT   │  │OTHCONTACT│
    │          │  │PHONE     │      Join
    │          │  │FAX       │
    │          │  │OTHPHONE  │      Unjoin
    │          │  │TYPE      │
    │          │  │SUBJECT   │      Options...
    │          │  │FAXFROM   │
    │          │  │PAGES     │      Print
    │          │  │ACCTNO    │
    │          │  │SHIPADDRS │
    │          │  │SHIPCITY  │
    │          │  │SHIPST    │
    │          │  │SHIPZIP   │
    │          │  │SHIPATTN  │
    └──────────┘  └──────────┘
    File: H:\APPROACH\SAMPLES\SPORTS\CUST.DBF
    Field:              Type:           Width:
```

Figure 23.2 The Join dialog box displaying two databases.

The two databases you opened are now "joined" at the fields you selected. When you change any information in one of these joined fields in either database, Approach will automatically update the other database.

If you want to unjoin two databases, click on the lines displayed between the database fields in the Join dialog box (to highlight them). Then click on the Unjoin button.

If you have more than one record with the same field contents (people's last names, for example), you might want to join both the last name fields and the first name fields. By doing this, you ensure that Approach doesn't *automatically* change every record with the last name of "Smith," for example.

> **Other Options** Click on the Options button to see more ways you can join databases. Don't forget: you can join many fields across several databases!

Lesson 23

Joining Records with Repeating Panels

If you have databases that store recurring data—for example, several customer orders per customer or multiple line items for each customer order—you can ask Approach to show you the information in a repeating panel.

> **Plain English**
> **Repeating Panel** The display of related, detail information found in a second database.

Let's use this example: You run a business that makes regular calls to customers, both for sales and follow-up. Whichever reason you're calling for, you need a way to see a list of all calls that have been made to a single customer. You'll need two databases in a single Approach file: one that holds customer information, and one that holds information about the calls made. You'll then create a single form that shows the general customer info along with a sorted list of all calls made to that customer.

In these steps, we're going to assume you've already created these two databases in your Approach file.

1. Open the Approach file that contains one of the databases you want to use.

2. Select Form from the Create menu. The Form Assistant dialog box opens (see Figure 23.3).

3. Fill in the information needed to create the form (as you learned in Lesson 16), but make sure you choose Standard with Repeating Panel as the SmartMaster layout.

4. Click on the Next>> button to continue.

Joining Files

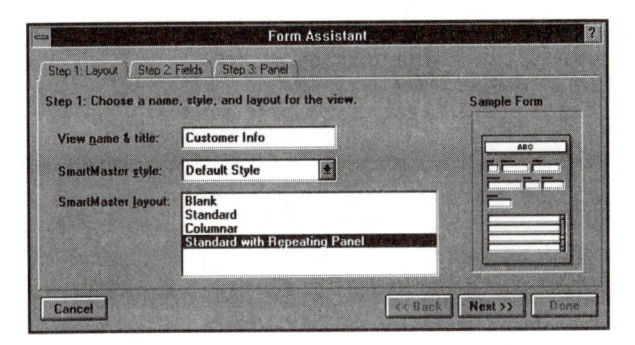

Figure 23.3 The Form Assistant dialog box.

5. Select the database that has the main or general info in it by clicking on the down arrow next to the Database fields text box. Since we're going to list calls made to customers, we'll choose our Customer database first.

6. Hold down the Ctrl key while clicking field names, until you've selected all the ones you want to use. Click on the >>Add>> button, and then click on the Next>> button.

7. Now select the fields to list on the repeating panel part of the form. This is the detail about all calls made to customers. Select the database that holds itemized call information, select the fields you want to see on your repeating panel, and click on the >>Add button.

8. Click on the Done button to see your new form created.

Figure 23.4 shows the form created using this set of steps. I fancied it up a bit with the techniques covered in Lessons 17 through 19.

Lesson 23

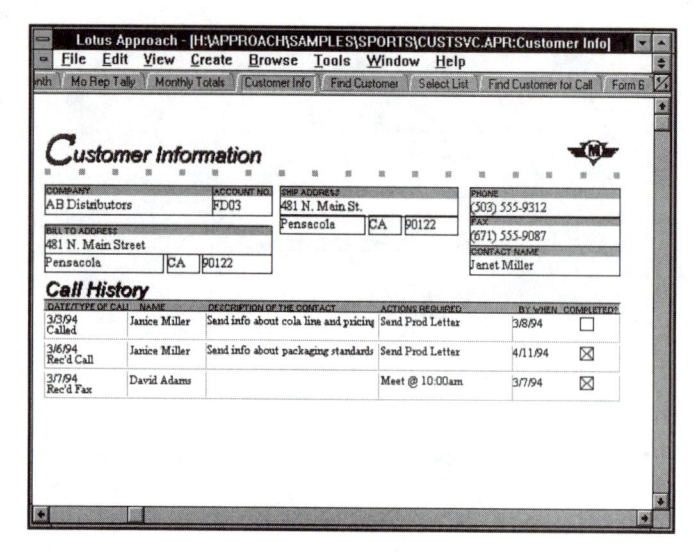

Figure 23.4 A sample form that displays detail from a joined database.

In this lesson you learned about joining database files to make your information work more effectively for you. In the next lesson, you'll learn how to create macros.

Lesson 24

Running Macros to Save Time

In this lesson, you'll learn how to create macros that automate your redundant tasks.

You can shave a lot of time off your daily workload if you create macros. A *macro* is a group of actions that are stored as a set, so you can just run that set of commands instead of running each command individually.

If you print reports based on information that's constantly being updated, such as the status of customer orders, for example, you'd do well to create a macro that will do it all for you. You have to run the macro to get the job done, but at least you don't have to go through every step in your process, over and over again—on a daily basis!

Creating New Macros

The following steps show how to create a macro.

1. Open an Approach file.
2. Select Macros from the Tools menu. The Macro dialog box opens (see Figure 24.1).

Lesson 24

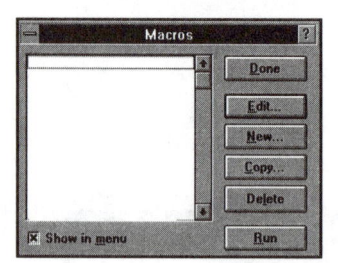

Figure 24.1 The Macros dialog box.

3. Click on the New button. The Define Macro dialog box opens, as in Figure 24.2.

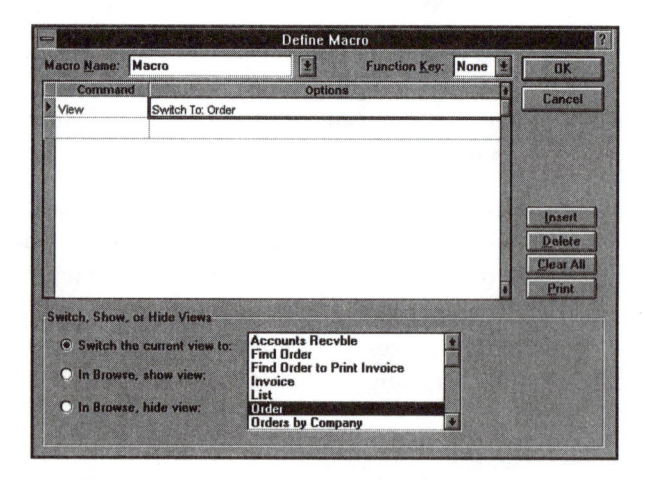

Figure 24.2 The Define Macro dialog box.

4. Name your new macro in the Macro Name text box. If you want to run your new macro from a function key, select a function key to run the macro from those listed in the Function Key list box. Function keys previously assigned will not appear on the list.

> **Make It Easy!** If you choose the name "open," your new macro will run as soon as you open the Approach file it's associated with.

Running Macros to Save Time   145

5. Click on the empty cell below the word "Command," and then click on the down arrow to see a list of available commands. Select one from the list.

> **Your Options** The lower half of the Define Macro dialog box shows you options that differ for each command.

6. Select any options for that command that appear in the lower half of the dialog box. If any dialog boxes appear requesting more information, complete them and select OK to continue.

7. Click on the next cell below the command you just chose, and select the next command to run.

8. Continue steps 6 and 7 until you're finished defining the macro. Figure 24.3 shows you my list of commands just before I saved my macro.

9. Click on the OK button to save your new macro.

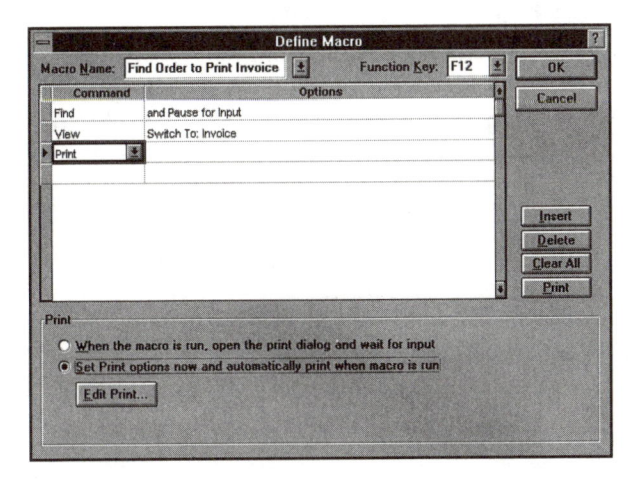

Figure 24.3 My finished macro.

When you save your new macro, it will appear on the new list displayed in the Macros dialog box. The next time you want to perform that set of actions, you simply press the function key that you assigned to the macro. (For example, all I have to do is press the F12 key to have Approach find a record and then print an invoice.)

Using Existing Macros

Approach comes with macros that exemplify what can be done with a well planned macro. You'll find sample Approach files in the /APPROACH/SAMPLES directory. These Approach files already include macros so you can get an idea of what can be done with macros.

> **Learn by Doing!** You might want to run these sample macros to see what they do, and then edit them further to customize them. Sometimes it's a lot easier to change an existing macro to fit your needs than it is to create one from scratch.

Here's how you run a macro:

1. Open the Approach file of choice.

2. Select Run Macro from Approach's Tools menu. Another menu opens, listing the available macros that you can run. If more macros exist than can be displayed on the menu, you'll see an item called More Macros. Select More Macros to see a dialog box that shows them all.

3. Select a macro and click OK. It runs.

Editing a Macro

Earlier, I suggested that you edit an existing macro instead of creating one from scratch. Let's edit a macro to make it do

Running Macros to Save Time 147

something a little differently. Here's how you edit an Approach macro:

1. Make sure you've opened the Approach file that holds the macro you want to edit.

2. Select Macros from the Tools menu. The Macros dialog box opens (Figure 24.4).

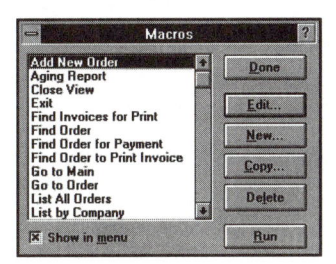

Figure 24.4 The Macros dialog box.

3. Click on a macro to select it, and then click on the Edit button to open the Define Macro dialog box (shown in Figure 24.5).

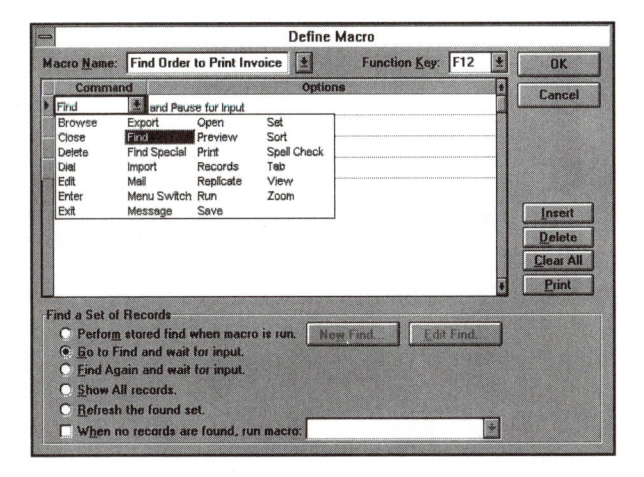

Figure 24.5 The Define Macro dialog box.

4. Click on one of the commands. Options for it appear in the bottom half of the dialog box. Change any options as desired.

5. If you want to delete a command, click on it, and then click on the Delete button.

6. If you want to add a command, click on the command above where you want to insert the new command. Then click the Insert button and add the command as you did when you created the macro.

7. Click on the OK button. Then click on the Done button to complete your changes.

When we run our edited macro, it will select all records and print out invoices for them all instead of finding a single record and then printing just the one invoice.

In this lesson, you learned to create and edit macros.

Appendix A

SmartIcons

The following table shows all the SmartIcons available in Approach and the purpose of each. For a quick look at only the SmartIcons on the default palette, see the inside back cover of this book.

SmartIcon	Description
	Add an empty space
	Create a new database file
	Open a file
	Save an Approach file
	Close a file
	Print the current view
	Print the current view
	Print the current form
	Configure the printer
	Exit Approach

continues

Appendix A

SmartIcon	Description
	Undo last change
	Cut
	Copy
	Paste
	Paste Special
	Design mode
	Design mode
	Browse mode
	Browse mode
	Preview
	Preview
	Go to the first record
	Go to the previous record
	Go to the next record
	Go to the last record
	Find a set of records
	Find a set of records

SmartIcons

SmartIcon	Description
	Find all records
	Find all records
	Find duplicate or unique records
	Sort
	Sort fields ascending
	Sort fields descending
	Find
	Delete a record
	Delete a record
	Create a new record
	Create a new record
	Duplicate a record
	Insert the time
	Insert today's date
	Duplicate previous record
	Import database

continues

Appendix A

SmartIcon	Description
	Export database
	Create a form
	Create a report
	Create a mailing label
	Create a form letter
	Create a worksheet
	Create a crosstab
	Create a chart
	Check spelling
	Send mail
	Show view tabs
	Open help
	Customize SmartIcons
	Next SmartIcon bar
	Run 1-2-3 for Windows
	Run Ami Pro for Windows
	Run Freelance for Windows

SmartIcons

SmartIcon	Description
	Run Organizer for Windows
	Run Notes for Windows
	Run Improv for Windows
	Run CC:Mail for Windows
	Run SmartPics for Windows

The following icons are the design tools that appear in a floating box when you are working in Design mode.

Tool	Description
	Selection pointer
	Enter text
	Make rectangle
	Make ellipse
	Make rounded rectangle
	Make line
	Make a field
	Make a check box
	Make a radio button

continues

Appendix A

Tool	Description
	Make a macro button
	Make a PicturePlus field
	Add a field

Appendix B

Windows Primer

Microsoft Windows is an interface program that makes your computer easier to use by enabling you to select menu items and pictures so you don't have to type commands. Before you can take advantage of it, however, you must learn some Windows basics.

Starting Microsoft Windows

To start Windows, do the following:

1. At the DOS prompt, type win.

2. Press Enter.

The Windows title screen appears for a few moments, and then you see a screen like the one in Figure B.1.

> **What If It Didn't Work?** You may have to change to the Windows directory before starting Windows; to do so, type CD \WINDOWS and press Enter.

Appendix B

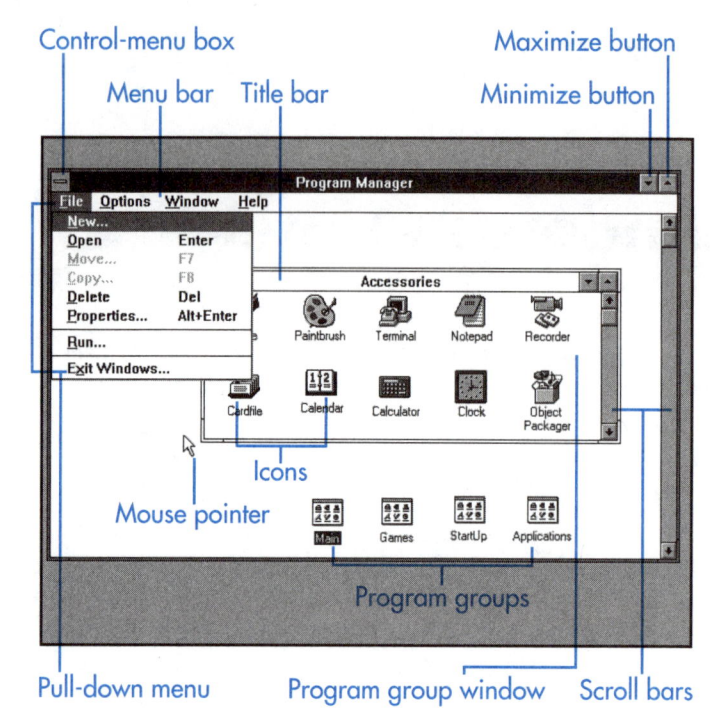

Figure B.1 The Windows Program Manager.

Using a Mouse

To work most efficiently in Windows, you should use a mouse. You can press mouse buttons and move the mouse in various ways to change the way it acts:

Point means to move the mouse pointer onto the specified item by moving the mouse. The tip of the mouse pointer must be touching the item.

Click on an item means to move the pointer onto the specified item and press the mouse button once. Unless specified otherwise, use the left mouse button.

Windows Primer

Double-click on an item means to move the pointer onto the specified item and press and release the left mouse button twice quickly.

Drag means to move the mouse pointer onto the specified item, hold down the mouse button, and move the mouse while holding down the button.

Figure B.2 shows how to use the mouse to perform common Windows activities, including running applications and moving and resizing windows.

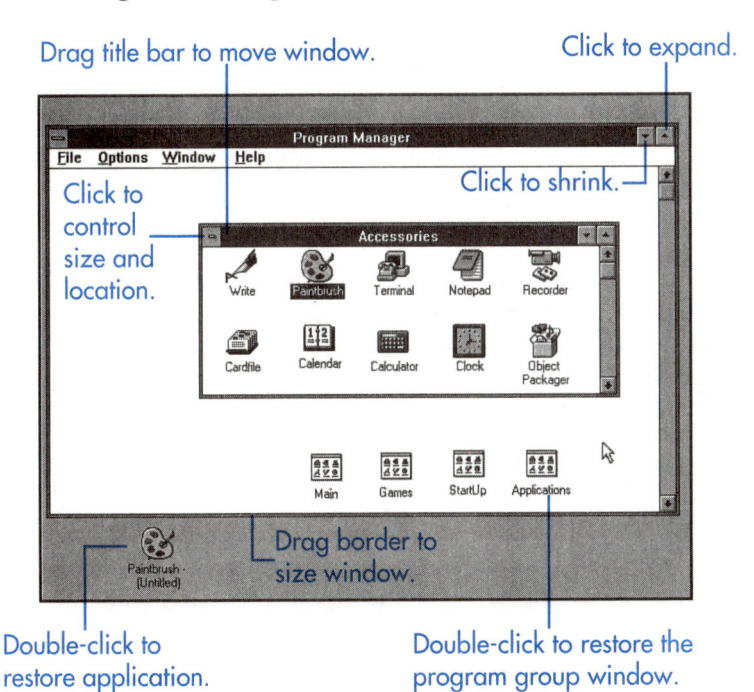

Figure B.2 Use your mouse to control Windows.

Appendix B

Starting a Program

To start a program, simply select its icon. If its icon is contained in a program group window that's not open at the moment, open the window first. Follow these steps:

1. If necessary, open the program group window that contains the program you want to run. To open a program group window, double-click on its icon.

2. Double-click on the icon for the program you want to run.

Using Menus

The menu bar contains various pull-down menus (see Figure B.3) from which you can select commands. Each Windows program that you run has a set of pull-down menus; Windows itself has a set too.

To open a menu, click on its name on the menu bar. Once a menu is open, you can select a command from it by clicking on the desired command.

Usually, when you select a command, the command is performed immediately. However:

- If the command name is gray (instead of black), the command is unavailable at the moment, and you cannot choose it.

- If the command name is followed by an arrow, selecting the command will cause another menu to appear, from which you must select another command.

- If the command name is followed by an ellipsis (three dots), selecting it will cause a dialog box to appear. You'll learn about dialog boxes in the next section.

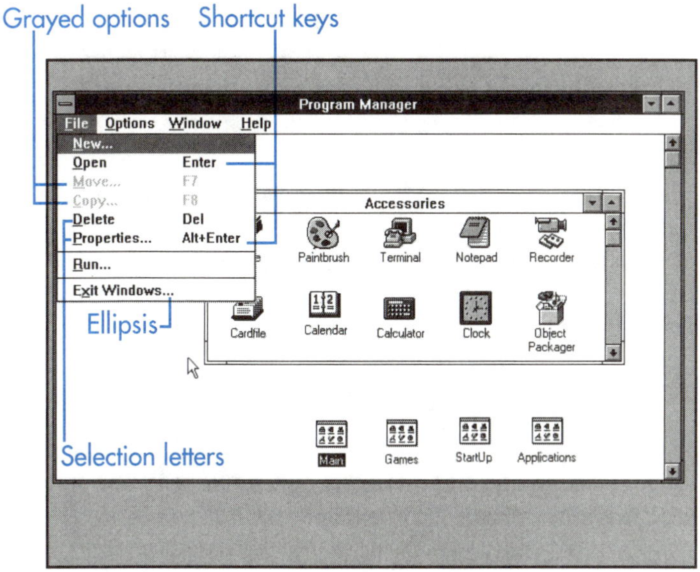

Figure B.3 A pull-down menu lists various commands you can perform.

Navigating Dialog Boxes

A dialog box is Windows' way of requesting additional information. For example, if you choose Print from the File menu of the Write application, you'll see the dialog box shown in Figure B.4.

Each dialog box contains one or more of the following elements:

List boxes display available choices. To activate a list, click inside the list box. If the entire list is not visible, use the scroll bar to view the items in the list. To select an item from the list, click on it.

Appendix B

Drop-down lists are similar to list boxes, but only one item in the list is shown. To see the rest of the items, click on the down arrow to the right of the list box. To select an item from the list, click on it.

Text boxes enable you to type an entry. To activate a text box, click inside it. To edit an existing entry, use the arrow keys to move the cursor and the Del or Backspace keys to delete existing characters. Then type your correction.

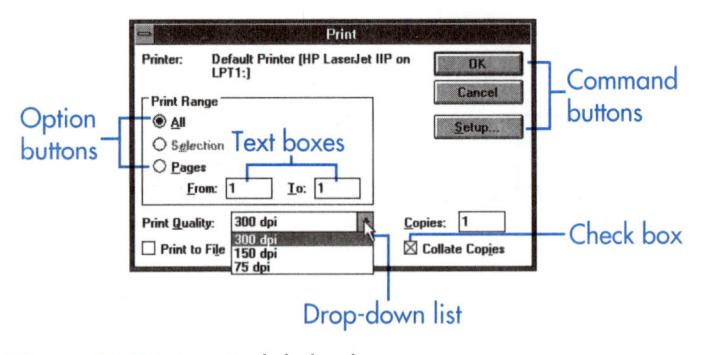

Figure B.4 A typical dialog box.

Check boxes enable you to select one or more items in a group of options. For example, if you are styling text, you can select Bold and Italic to have the text appear in both bold and italic type. Click on a check box to activate it.

Option buttons are like check boxes, but you can select only one option button in a group. Selecting one button unselects any option that is already selected. Click on an option button to activate it.

Command buttons execute (or cancel) the command once you have made your selections in the dialog box. To press a command button, click on it.

Switching Between Windows

Many times you will have more than one window open at once. Some open windows may be program group windows, while others may be actual programs that are running. To switch among them, you can:

- Pull down the Window menu and choose the window you want to view

    Or

- If a portion of the desired window is visible, click on it.

Controlling a Window

As you saw earlier in this appendix, you can minimize, maximize, and restore windows on your screen. But you can also move them and change their size.

- To move a window, drag its title bar to a different location. (Remember, drag means to hold down the left mouse button while you move the mouse.)

- To resize a window, position the mouse pointer on the border of the window until you see a double-headed arrow; then drag the window border to the desired size.

Index

Symbols
3-D charts, 88-90

A
Add Field dialog box, 132
adding records (databases), 59-61
Align command (Object menu), 119
Align dialog box, 119
aligning fields (forms), 117-119
Approach File Info command (File menu), 42
Approach File Info dialog box, 43
Arrange command (Objects menu), 111
arranging SmartIcons, 20
Ascending Sort SmartIcon, 71
attributes (objects), 101-102
Auto-Attach, 3

B
bars (SmartIcons), 21-22
Browse command (View menu), 36, 102, 121
Browse mode, 36, 59
Browse SmartIcon, 36, 59, 102
bubble help, 24-25

C
calculated fields, 128-132
Chart Assistant dialog box, 89
Chart command (Create menu), 88
charts, 3-4, 35-36, 88-90
Choose Key Fields dialog boxes, 57
clicking mouse, 156-157
Clipboard (graphics), 108
columns, 1-2
Contents command (Help menu), 25-26
context sensitive help, 23-24
Convert To dialog box, 48
Creating New Database dialog box, 38
crosstabs, summarizing, 126-128
customizing
  reports, 76-77
  SmartIcon Bar, 18
  sorting, 72-73
Cut command (Edit menu), 107
cutting graphics, 107

D
data entry (minimizing errors), 133
databases, 1-2, 37-42
  Auto-Attach, 3
  calculated fields, 129-132

Index

data entry, 133
fields, 1-2
files, joining, 137-139
flat-file, 137
forms, 2, 92-95
naming, 37-42
records, 2, 59-61
relational, 137
reports, 74-77
saving, 40, 40-42
sharing information, 2-3
software, 137
sorting, 69-70
templates, 37
worksheets, 77-78
Default SmartIcons, 16-22
Define Macro dialog box, 144
Define Radio Buttons dialog box, 117
Delete Found Set command (Browse menu), 68
Delete Record command (Browse menu), 67
Delete Sets dialog box, 21
Delete SmartIcon, 68
deleting
    graphics, 108
    multiple records, 68
    records, 67-68
    SmartIcon sets, 20-21
    text, 101
delimiter characters (fields), 57-58
Descending Sort SmartIcon, 71
Design command (View menu), 36, 76, 96
Design mode, 36
    entering, 96-97
    exiting, 102
    objects, 97
    text, 101-102
    tools icons, 153-154
    Tools palette, 103
Design SmartIcon, 36, 76, 96
dragging mouse, 156-157
drawing graphics, 103-106

E

editing
    macros, 146-148
    text, 101-102
embedding objects, 109-112

entering Design mode, 96-97
errors (data entry), 133
Exit & Return command (File menu), 109
Exit command (File menu), 9
exiting Design mode, 102
Export Data command (File menu), 56
Export Data dialog box, 56
exporting, 55-57
    to text file, 57-58
    to word processor, 57-58

F

Field Definitions command (Create menu), 39, 129, 135
Field Definitions dialog box, 40, 130, 135
field names (forms), 91
Field Names dialog box, 47, 55
fields, 1-2, 39-40
    calculated, 128-132
    delimiter characters, 57-58
    formatting InfoBoxes, 115-116
    forms, aligning, 117-119
    order, 113-114
    repeating panel, 94
    selecting, 118
    tab key, 113-114
    validating, 133-136
files
    databases, 37-42
    information, 42-43
    joining, 137-139
    opening, 44-51
    password protection, 41-42
    text, opening, 49-51
    view tabs, 14-15
Find command (Browse menu), 63
Find SmartIcon, 63
flat-file databases, 137
footers, 5-6
Form Assistant dialog box, 92
Form command (Create menu), 92
Form Letter Assistant dialog box, 82
Form Letter command (Create menu), 82
form letters, 5, 34-35, 82-87
Form view, sorting, 71
formatting fields (InfoBoxes), 115-116

forms, 1-2, 91-95
    fields
        aligning, 117-119
        calculated, 128-132
        items, selecting, 94
        records (repeating panels), 140
        validated fields, 133
        views, 2-3
forms view, 31-36, 59
formulas (calculated fields),
    131-132

G

graphics
    cutting, 107
    deleting, 108
    drawing, 103-106
    importing, 106-107
    OLE (object linking and
        embedding), 108-110
    print quality, 123
    stacking, 111-112

H

handles (objects), 98
headers, 5-6
help
    bubble, 24-25
    context-sensitive, 23-24
    F1 key, 23-24
    jump words, 26
    Help menu, 25-29
Help menu commands
    Contents, 25-26
    Search, 27
Help SmartIcon, 26

I

icons
    design tools, 153-154
    SmartIcons, 16-22
Import Data command (File menu),
    53
Import Data dialog box, 53
Import Setup dialog box, 53
importing, 52-55
    graphics, 106-107
    worksheet data, 55
InfoBox, 101
InfoBoxes, 101, 115-116
Insert Object dialog box, 109
items (forms), 94

J-K

Join command (Create menu), 138
Join dialog box, 138
joining
    files, 137-139
    records and repeating panels,
        140-142
jump words, 26

L

labels, mailing, 79-81
letters, 5
letters (form), 34-35, 82-87
linking objects, 109-112
Lotus Approach
    quiting, 9-10
    starting, 7-9

M

macros, 143-146
    editing, 146-148
    running, 146
Macros command (Tools menu),
    143
Macros dialog box, 144
Mailing Label Assistant dialog box,
    80
Mailing Label command (Create
    menu), 80
mailing labels, 4-5, 79-81
menu bar, 12-13
menus, 158-159
modes
    Browse, 36
    Design, 36
modifying records, 67
mouse, 156-157
    objects
        moving, 99
        sizing, 100
moving
    objects, 99
    SmartIcon Bar, 21-22
    windows, 161

N

naming databases, 37-42
navigating dialog boxes, 159-160
New command (File menu), 37
New dialog box, 37
New Record command (Browse
    menu), 60

Index

New Record SmartIcon, 60
numbers, summarizing, 126-128

O

Object command (Create menu), 108
Object menu commands
 Align, 119
 Arrange, 111
objects, 97
 attributes, 101-102
 embedding, 109-112
 handles, 98
 linking, 109-112
 moving, 99
 OLE (object linking and embedding), 108-109
 resizing, 100
OLE (object linking and embedding)
 graphics, 108-110
 objects, 108-109
Open command (File menu), 14, 44
Open dialog box, 45
Open SmartIcon, 44
opening
 files, 44-51
 text files, 49-51
 worksheets, 47-48

P

palettes (Tools), 103
password protection, 41-42
Paste command (Edit menu), 107
Paste from File command (Edit menu), 106
Paste from File dialog box, 106
pasting graphics, 107
pointing mouse, 156-157
Preview command (File menu), 85, 120
previewing printing, 120-121
Print command (File menu), 86, 122
Print dialog box, 122
Print Setup commands (File menu), 124
Print Setup dialog box, 124
printing
 graphics (quality), 123
 previewing, 120-121
 setup, 123-125
 views, 121-123
programs, starting, 158

Q-R

quiting Lotus Approach, 9-10
radio buttons, 116-117
records
 calculated fields, 128-132
 changing, 67
 databases, 2, 59-61
 deleting, 67-68
 finding, 62-66
  multiple, 64-68
  SmartIcons, 65-68
 repeating panels (joining), 140-142
relational databases, 137
repeating panels
 (fields), 94
 joining records, 140-142
Report Assistant dialog box, 75
Report command (Create menu), 74
report views, 33-34
reports, 74-77
 customizing, 76-77
 headers/footers, 5-6
rows, 1-2
Run Macro command (Tools menu), 146
running macros, 146

S

Save Approach File command (File menu), 41
Save Approach File dialog box, 41
Save Set of SmartIcons dialog box, 19
Save SmartIcon, 41
saving databases, 40-42
screen, 11-13
 menu bar, 12-13
 SmartIcons, 13
 status bar, 13
 title bar, 12
Search command (Help menu), 27
Search dialog box, 27
searches
 multiple records, 64-68
 records, 62-66
selecting
 fields, 118
 items (forms), 94
 SmartIcons, 17-18
selection handles (objects), 98
setup (printing), 123-125

Show Data Entry Order command
  (View menu), 113
Show Status Bar command (View
  menu), 86
sizing
  objects, 100
  SmartIcons, 22
  windows, 161
SmartIcons, 13, 16-22, 149-154
  arranging, 20
  Ascending Sort, 71
  Browse, 36, 59, 102
  Delete, 68
  Descending Sort, 71
  Design, 36, 76, 96
  Find, 63
  Help, 26
  New Record, 60
  Open, 44
  records, 65-68
  Save, 41
  sets, 18-21
  sizing, 22
SmartIcons bar, 18, 21-22
SmartIcons command (Tools
  menu), 18
SmartIcons dialog box, 18
software (databases), 137
Sort command (Browse menu), 71
Sort dialog box, 73
sorting
  customized, 72-73
  databases, 69-70
  Form view, 71
  Worksheet view, 71-72
stacking graphics, 111-112
starting
  Lotus Approach, 7-9
  programs, 158
  Windows, 7-9, 155-156
status bar, 13
summarizing quantities, 126-128
Summary command (Create menu),
  127
Summary dialog box, 127
switching between windows, 161

T

tab key (fields), 113-114
tables, 1-2
tabs (view tabs), 30-36
templates, 37
text (Design mode), 101-102
Text File Options dialog box, 50,
  58

text files
  exporting to, 57-58
  opening, 49-51
  Text-Delimited file, 49
  Text-Fixed Length, 49
title bar, 12
Tools palette (Design mode), 103

U-V

Update command (File menu), 109

validated fields, 133, 135-136
view tabs, 14-15
views, 30-36
  Browse mode, 36
  charts, 35-36
  Design mode, 36
  form letters, 34-35
  forms, 2-3, 31-36
  modes, 36
  printing, 121-123
  report, 33-34
  worksheet, 32-33

W-Z

Welcome to Lotus Approach dialog
  box, 9
Windows, starting, 7-9, 155-156
windows, 161
word processors, 57-58
Worksheet Assistant dialog box, 77
Worksheet command (Create
  menu), 77
worksheet views, 32-33, 71-72
worksheets, 4
  creating, 77-78
  importing data, 55
  opening, 47-48
  summarizing, 126-128